HEILSGESCHICHTE
AS A MODEL FOR
BIBLICAL THEOLOGY

Heilsgeschichte as a Model for Biblical Theology

The Debate Concerning the Uniqueness and Significance of Israel's Worldview

Robert Gnuse

COLLEGE THEOLOGY SOCIETY
STUDIES IN RELIGION • 4

UNIVERSITY
PRESS OF
AMERICA

Lanham • New York • London

Copyright © 1989 by

The College Theology Society

University Press of America, ® Inc.

4720 Boston Way
Lanham, MD 20706

3 Henrietta Street
London WC2E 8LU England

Printed in the United States of America

British Cataloging in Publication Information Available

Co-published by arrangement with
The College Theology Society

Library of Congress Cataloging–in–Publication Data

Gnuse, Robert Karl, 1947–
Heilsgeschichte as a model for biblical theology : the debate
concerning the uniqueness and significance of Israel's worldview /
Robert Gnuse.
p.   cm.
(College Theology Society studies in religion ; 4)
"Co-published by arrangement with the College Theology Society"–
–T.p. verso.
Bibliography: p.
Includes indexes.
1. Bible. O.T.– –Historiography. 2. History (Theology)– –Biblical
teaching. 3. Historiography– –Middle East. I Title. II. Series.
BS1197.G58   1988   88–39923 CIP
221.9'5– –dc19
ISBN 0–8191–7245–6 (alk. paper).
ISBN 0–8191–7246–4 (pbk. : alk. paper)

All University Press of America books are produced on acid-free paper.
The paper used in this publication meets the minimum requirements of American
National Standard for Information Sciences—Permanence of Paper for Printed Library
Materials, ANSI Z39.48–1984.   ∞

Contents

v

Editor's Preface

The College Theology Society co-publishes CTS Studies In Religion with University Press of America. The CTS Studies series is one of three series reflecting the scholarly and pedagogical interests of the Society's membership. This series is devoted to the publication of original monographs which make a significant contribution to contemporary theological reflection. The Resources Series includes anthologies, translations and textbooks, while the Reprint Series reissues books which are of significant value for the classroom. The College Theology Society is a professional organization of college and university professors numbering over 800 members in all fifty states, Canada and Europe.

The Research and Publications Committee of the CTS has sole editorial responsibility for the selection, design and production of CTS Resources in Religion, CTS Studies in Religion and CTS Reprints in Religion. Further information regarding these series can be obtained from the Editor. The sales and distribution of the volumes in these three series are the responsibility of University Press of America.

The editors are grateful for the work of Dr. Bernard Batto in the preparation of this manuscript, as well as to Ms. Maylon Englund for assistance in the manuscript revision.

Managing Editor
James Gaffney
Loyola University
New Orleans, LA 70118

Chair Publications Committee
Robert Masson (outgoing)
Marquette University
Milwaukee, WI 53233

John McCarthy
Loyola University of Chicago
Chicago, IL 60626

To
Karl Arthur Gnuse (1913–   )
and
Frances Rupp Gnuse (1915–   )

Chapter 1
The Concept of Salvation History

In the past generation it was commonplace for biblical theologians to speak of the central theme in the Scriptures as one which described God acting in the historical affairs of people. The Exodus and Resurrection were perceived not only as the central theological symbols in the Bible but as paradigmatic for how God interacted with humanity in general, through the course of human events.

These two events were divine irruptions into the flow of history which altered human experience. Other events in the Bible were seen in similar fashion, so that the entire text was described as a coherent and unified testimony to the continual actions of a gracious God in the sphere of human history.

Hence, the term "salvation history" or the German term, *Heilsgeschichte,* was used increasingly to describe the entire biblical tradition.[1] Some theologians even extended the notion to the general concept of revelation *in totu,* so that all history was perceived as the process of divine revelation.[2] Most biblical theologians, however, remained cautious and distinguished *Heilsgeschichte* from *Weltgeschichte,* the former sequence of events was apprehended by faith while the latter was empirical, observable history.

Within the recent generation this theological model has come under serious criticism from philosophers of history, theologians, exegetes, and historians. The points of attack were several:

1) Not all the biblical material seemed to have a "historical orientation." Psalms, legal texts, and Wisdom Literature

1

(Proverbs, Koheleth, and Job) appear quite timeless in comparison to the narrative materials.

2) History was never clearly defined as a theological or philosophical category by the biblical theologians. Modern notions of historiography were imputed to ancient Israel, when they did not even possess a word for history. Israel's historiographical skills were lauded not only over ancient Near Eastern contemporaries but even over the later Greek historians.

3) Distinctions between various definitions of history were not maintained consistently. The events perceived quite subjectively by faith were described frequently as though they were simple, objective, observable events. Terms such as *Geschichte* (popular or interpreted history) and *Historie* (real, scientific, factual history) were introduced by theologians. Biblical accounts were called *Geschichte*, but then unconsciously regarded as *Historie* by some theologians.

4) The relationship between the actual salvific events and the later interpretations of the primal events, which were also found in the text, was never resolved. Gerhard von Rad and Rudolf Bultmann indicated that from their viewpoint the events were less significant than the interpretations built upon them. They implied that historical facticity of the original events was unimportant in the light of the later interpretations, for these often displaced any memory of the original event in the text. This raised the spectre of theology and faith built upon a sheer fabrication in the opinion of many critics. Von Rad seemed to imply two levels of history: what really happened and what was later confessed in the traditions.

5) Unfair comparisons were made with the contemporary ancient Near Eastern modes of thought. The contrast was designed to highlight the uniqueness of the Israelite way of thinking, but often scholarly objectivity was sacrificed. The paradigm was pedagogical and had as its goal certain theological agenda for the modern Church. But the result was an unfair and subjective portrayal.

It is this last observation which this work wishes to treat in further detail. The comparison between the ancient Near East and Israel has gone through two diametrically opposed stages of evaluation since World War II. First, the biblical theologians with their "salvation history" emphasis stressed the radical differences between the two cultures; then, their critics of a more recent era have emphasized the continuity between the two cultures.

A more realistic appraisal, I believe, lies between these two opinions. Israel may be different, but not unique, in relation to ancient Near Eastern predecessor cultures. Israel took latent ideas found in the ancient Near East and put them together in a new construal which brought previously unemphasized perspectives to the fore. This reconstruction of ancient Near Eastern thought caused the emergence of new attitudes in social, political, and economic perceptions, as well as the religious dimension.[3] Israelites did not break with ancient Near Eastern values; rather they were heirs of a great heritage with which they effected a creative advance, an evolutionary move forward, in the reconstruction of those values.

When we speak of Israel, we are not describing phenomenologically the entire culture or all the people, but rather that revolutionary vanguard of Yahwistic prophets and priests whose minority religious views prevailed at last only with the Babylonian exile of the sixth century B.C. Throughout Israel's pre-exilic history this group constituted a minority.

Our study shall consider the progression of scholarship on the issue of salvation history as a theologomena in the Hebrew Bible over the past two generations of biblical studies. We shall first consider the views of a generation of salvation history theologians. Then we shall examine in greater detail the critical response levelled against this position. Attention shall be given to the general theological critiques, the evaluation of historiography in Israel and the ancient world, the comparison of salvation history themes in both cultures, and the reassessment of religious continuity between Israel and the ancient Near East. The continuing debate over the last twenty years between advocates of both positions shall be briefly reviewed. We shall then turn our consideration to possible

3

ways in which to speak of salvation history and Israel's world-view in the light of contemporary scholarly discussion. Not only the way in which Israel diverged from surrounding cultures but also the causes for that development will be reviewed; herein lies another complex debate. Finally, we shall offer some suggestions for future discussion. These must not be viewed as final but rather as tentative suggestions designed to stimulate further discussion. As often is the case, answers cannot be given to questions of ideological or theological significance, especially when dealing with cultures and literature created thousands of years ago. We simply have too many lacunae in our understandings. We must never forget that our theories will remain tentative constructs designed to help us perceive the past for the sake of the present. We must always be ready to reassess our theories for the sake of integrating new data and insights for a better perspective. The suggestions provided by this monograph offer a nuance in the range of opinions which may help us move toward a new consensus.

Notes

1. George Ernest Wright, *God Who Acts: Biblical Theology as Recital,* Studies in Biblical Theology, vol. 8 (London: SCM, 1952), pp. 12–32, and "From the Bible to the Modern World," *Biblical Authority for Today,* eds. Alan Richardson and Wolfgang Schweitzer (London: SCM, 1951), pp. 219–239, as well as other essays in this work; Wright and Reginald Fuller, *The Book of the Acts of God* (Garden City: Doubleday, 1957), pp. 27–38 et passim; Norman Snaith, *The Inspiration and Authority of the Bible* (London: Epworth, 1956), pp. 9–46; Charles Harold Dodd, *The Authority of the Bible,* rev. ed. (London: Fontana, 1960), pp. 216–219, 257–263; Richardson, *The Bible in the Age of Science* (Philadelphia: Westminster, 1961), pp. 122–141, provides a good summary of Wright, Dodd, and Oscar Cullmann; Henning Graf Reventlow, *Problems of Old Testament Theology in the Twentieth Century* (Philadelphia: Fortress, 1985), pp. 87–91, provides a thorough bibliography on salvation history, and on pp. 59–124 overviews the greater issues of the Bible as history; and Robert Gnuse, *The Authority of the Bible* (New York: Paulist, 1985),

pp. 66–74, evaluates salvation history as a way to understand biblical authority.

2. Wolfhart Pannenberg, "Hermeneutics and Universal History," trans. Paul Achtemeier, *History and Hermeneutic,* Journal for Theology and the Church, vol. 4, eds. Robert Funk and Gerhard Ebeling (New York: Harper and Row, 1967), pp. 122–152, and "Heilsgeschehen und Geschichte," *Kerygma und Dogma* 5 (1959): 218–237, 259–288; Rolf Rendtorff, "Hermeneutik des Alten Testaments als Frage nach Geschichte," *Zeitschrift für Theologie und Kirche* 57 (1960): 27–40; and Jürgen Moltmann, *Theology of Hope,* trans. James Leitch (New York: Harper and Row, 1975), pp. 15–388. The truly significant source is a collection of essays: R. Rendtorff, "The Concept of Revelation in Ancient Israel," pp. 25–53, Ulrich Wilkens, "The Understanding of Revelation With the History of Primitive Christianity," pp. 57–121, Pannenberg, "Dogmatic Theses on the Doctrine of Revelation," pp. 125–158, and Trutz Rendtorff, "The Problem of Revelation in the Concept of the Church," pp. 161–181, *Revelation as History,* trans. David Granskou (New York: Macmillan, 1968), pp. 23–121.

3. Currently other scholars are making similar observations about Israel's reconstruction of ancient Near Eastern values: John Hayes, *Introduction to the Bible* (Philadelphia: Westminster, 1971), p. 136; Walter Brueggemann, "A Shape for Old Testament Theology, I: Structure Legitimation," *Catholic Biblical Quarterly* 47 (1985): 28–46, offers the most extensive discussion on this issue; Patrick Miller, "Israelite Religion," *The Hebrew Bible and its Modern Interpreters,* eds. Douglas Knight and Gene Tucker, The Bible and its modern interpreters, vol. 1 (Chico, California: Scholars Press, 1985), p. 107; and Shmuel Noah Eisenstadt, "The Axial Age Breakthrough in Ancient Israel," *The Origins and Diversity of Axial Age Civilizations,* ed. Eisenstadt, SUNY Series in Near Eastern Studies (Albany, New York: State University of New York, 1986), pp. 127–134.

5

Chapter 2
Advocates of Salvation History Theology

After World War II a biblical theological movement arose to extol the significance and meaning of the biblical traditions for doing theology. One of their points of departure was the comparison of ancient Near Eastern beliefs with an emphasis upon nature, myth, cult, and a cyclic view of reality against a linear view of reality emphasizing epics, law, and morality in Israelite belief. For pedagogical and ideological reasons these stereotypical distinctions were highlighted quite strongly in the discussion concerning the nature of biblical theology.[1]

Significant works by Old Testament scholars, New Testament scholars, and even ancient Near Eastern historians lauded the uniqueness of the Israelite (and later Christian) historical worldview and the ramifications resultant from such a perspective.[2] Biblical theologians used this construct not only in their evaluation of the biblical tradition but also as a starting point for interpreting individual texts throughout the Scriptures, for the development of hermeneutical models, a renewed interest in the typological approach, biblical theology, and Christian theology in general.[3]

A. Scholarly Exuberance

Voices on the continent first gave utterance to the contrast of cultures. Scholars compared the cyclic and nature oriented perspective of the ancient Near East with the linear and historically oriented perspective of Israel as the key to discovering Israel's unique theological or ideational contribution to the development of human thought.

German scholars provided the initial generalizations. Martin Noth at an early stage spoke of the contrast between Israel's thought and the surrounding world:

> In the religions of the ancient Oriental world we have a constantly recurring play of mythical forces, in which the superhuman control by the divine is observed and admired, whether it be in matters concerning heaven and earth, or the stars and the elements of life and death, whereas in the Old Testament it is chiefly the once occurring event which is understood as a divine manifestation.[4]

More recently we find the same perspective in Georg Fohrer's significant study of the history of Israel's religion:

> In this linkage with history we seem to see the true difference between Yahwism and other religions, with their timeless or non-historical basis, and thus the revelatory nature of Yahwism.[5]

Scandanavian scholars tended to be more sympathic to ancient Near Eastern cultures and were more inclined to see parallels with Israelite beliefs and customs, in part as a result of their deep interest in observations of the "Myth and Ritual" School of Ivan Engnell, Samuel Hooke, and others. But even among these scholars one can find the tendency to place Israelite and ancient Near Eastern beliefs in opposition. In several instances Sigmund Mowinckel made such observations:

> All the ancient religions and civilizations, even those of Greece, conceived of the course of history as a circle, corresponding to the annual cycle of the life of nature. The Old Testament conceives of history as a straight line, pointing to a goal.[6]

Though most of the previously mentioned scholars would be readily classified as quite critical, even the more theologically conservative scholars on the continent began to integrate these observations into their work. Typical of this stance is the conservative Reformed Dutch scholar, Theodore Vriezen:

> Israel did not derive its knowledge of God first and foremost from nature, as the ancient oriental peoples did, but from the acts of God in the history of the people.[7]

New Testament scholars followed the lead and made the same observations in Europe. The most well known in this regard is Oscar Cullmann, a person intimately associated with salvation history theology:

> . . . the symbol of time for Primitive Christianity as well as for Biblical Judaism and the Iranian religion is the upward sloping line, while in Hellenism it is the circle.[8]

The comparison was thus extended to the New Testament in contrast to the Greek or Hellenistic world view of the surrounding milieu.

After the war American biblical scholars would begin to use this imagery extensively and develop the comparison between cultures even more. Typical is the general observation formulated by Millar Burrows:

> Through all the ancient Israelite interpretations of history runs a consistent and characteristic understanding of time as proceeding in a straight line, with a beginning and an end. This is in sharp contrast with the ideas of history prevalent among many other people as consisting of an endless recurrence of cycles leading nowhere.[9]

George Ernest Wright, who would be the most articulate spokesperson for this position, could state:

> Polytheistic man, borne on the rhythmic cycle of nature, has no primary concern with history; instead his focus of attention is upon the yearly cycle in which life is recreated each spring and the blessing of order established. He is "bound in the bundle of life" with nature, which is the kingdom of the gods, and his existence moves with the natural rhythm. Biblical man was "bound in the bundle of life" with God who was not an immanence in nature but the Creator of nature.[10]

9

With Wright the stereotypical comparisons were articulated with vivid style and the theological implications were drawn forth most completely.

Biblical theologians so completely used this comparison that writers in other fields began to assume that the contrast was a given intellectual conclusion. Even a noted historian and philosopher of history, Herbert Butterfield, who was dependent upon biblical scholarship for his consideration of Hebrew historiography, would say that Israelites did not believe the world to be:

> . . . an aimless revolving, the wheels always on the move but everything remaining really in the same state. To them, history was not cyclic, but predominantly linear—irreversible and unrepeatable. (God) was still capable of doing new things . . . novelties in the process of time.[11]

The contrast between Israel and the ancient world appeared to be well established in scholarly circles.

B. Historiography

The discussion of revelation through history and salvation history naturally led to a consideration of historiographical materials. Israelites were credited with a high level of historiographic skill. This resulted from the experience of God in the flow of human events, for such divine presence generated the skills of history writing.[12] Scholars spoke of how Israel was unique in this regard; Israelites moved beyond their ancient Near Eastern contemporaries in terms of a historical perspective on reality.[13] This historiographical tradition developed out of a rich epic tradition, a type of oral tradition which lent itself most naturally to describing divine action in human affairs.

Israelite literature was compared to ancient historiography and the latter was found wanting. Ancient Near Eastern materials were called mere annals compared to the more fully developed epic narratives and historiography of Israel. Annals

10

were said to lack a sense of the unity of history and thus failed to provide an interpretation of history. The ancient Near East provided lists, genealogies, royal chronicles, military reports, eponym lists, king lists, accounts of heroic deeds, and other annalistic forms of records, but these were merely "raw material" for historiography. The ancients recorded only single events, they could not break out of their mythic oriented worldview to obtain a grand view of the greater course of history. Israelite historiography, however, encompassed more things and placed all people, not only kings, under the scrutiny of a grand moral assessment.[14] True history could not develop until ancient Near Eastern kingship was demythologized, according to some scholars, for only then could history be written about kings rather than by them, critique could replace royal propaganda. Israel did this because therein alone did a people create a popular monarchy perceived to be finite.[15]

Biblical theologians evaluated individual cultures and specific documents with a critical and condemnatory perspective. Egyptian historiography was characterized as static and changing little over the endless millennia, recording only the rules of various pharaohs, major events, and little more. Mesopotamians perceived the ebb and flow of various dynasties with a rhythmic regularity that suggested great cosmic laws, but they never developed history writing. The Weidner Chronicle and the Babylonian Chronicle were described as falling short of the high level of biblical historiography, such as the Deuteronomistic History. These were not serious attempts to write history. Mesopotamians might recapitulate historical data, but they lacked the over-arching themes and the promise-fulfillment perspective which occurred on a grand scale in the Hebrew Scriptures.[16]

Scholars began to laud the accomplishments of the Israelite authors. Their literature was described as an alien entity and an erratic insertion into the ideational traditions of the ancient world because the views contained therein were so radically advanced.[17] Biblical theologians were assured of their results,

11

and a great deal of literature was produced which built upon these observations. Alfred Jepsen could conclude:

> . . . the ancient orient knows no historical writing, which can be compared to the books of Kings, if one includes under historical writings a collected presentation of past events under a unified view of history. (author's translation)[18]

Even more boldly stated is Mowinckel's assessment:

> It is a well known fact, that Israel is the only people in the whole ancient Near East, where annalistic writing developed into real historiography. Neither the Babylonians nor the Assyrians took it beyond short chronicles in annalistic form; (they have) a boastful enumeration of glorious deeds.[19]

Not content with their denigrating comparisons with ancient Near Eastern materials, biblical scholars and others began to praise Israel as the inventor of history writing and the most significant culture for the promulgation of historiography in general. Herbert Butterfield offered this praise:

> There emerges a people not only supremely conscious of the past but possibly more obsessed with history than any other nation that has ever existed. The very key to its whole development seems to have been the power of its historical memory.[20]

Johannes Lindblom put it even more directly:

> The conclusion is inevitable: Israel was the pioneer of history-writing, and became so by virtue of its religion. Through the work and influence of prophets and prophetic personalities the art of history-writing was given to this people.[21]

Herodotus and Thucydides had to step aside as the great classical contributors to the rise of historiography, for now Israel was seen as the origin of history writing as we would come to know it eventually. Biblical scholars even began to denigrate the classical Greek historiographers directly. A classic example is again found Lindblom:

> Among the Greeks Herodotus describes many fascinating scenes from history, which, however, for the most part lack any close

12

and coherent sequence—they form a "dramatic series of pic-
tures," . . . Thucydides was indeed a forerunner of modern
history writing, but he did not understand how to write a
coherent national history or a world-history, and, moreover, he
was much later than the great Hebrew historical works.[22]

Such a strong assessment must have rankled classicists in
general and classical historians in particular. This boldness on
the part of biblical scholars assured that a counter-response
from the ancient Near Eastern scholars as well as classicists
would be forthcoming.

C. Cyclic-Linear Comparisons

These evaluations of Israel's historiographic skills were really a prelude to discussing Israelite values in other areas.
Israelite understandings were placed in opposition to contemporary ancient views on nature, myth, ritual, society, and
personal morality. Israel was said to be more ethical or moral
with a greater concern for social values, human relationships,
personal religion, and social change, because it was freed from
the cyclic world view with its emphasis upon nature religion.
The writings of George Ernest Wright best exemplified this
particular perspective, though his views were sometimes ster-
eotyped to the point of being simplistic. Many other scholars
used these same categories in their discussion with varying
degrees of sophistication.[23]

The primary contrast came in the perception of nature.
Ancient Near Eastern people were said to experience the
personal, direct, and throbbing presence of nature, that ani-
mate realm wherein the divine was experienced. Ancient people were caught in a cosmic interplay of forces into which they
must be integrated to survive. These natural forces were then
personified and sometimes deified. The natural cycles in the
physical realm inspired modes of description for the divine
realm. The gods were personifications of natural forces, expe-

13

rienced in the realm of nature and committed to pre-determined cycles of regular activity, as were the cycles of nature.[24]

By way of contrast Israelites regarded the natural order with less fear, for their single deity transcended the forces of nature. For them nature was a thing, an arena of human and divine activity, which received no sacred awe. Furthermore, they were placed above nature as the lords of the world, commissioned by God to rule in His stead (Genesis 1 says that they *radah,* "rule," the world). Hence, for them the important issue was not integration into the forces of nature but adjustment to the will of a God who had chosen them.[25]

The cyclic pattern in nature translated itself into the literary category of myth, stories which recounted the great archetypal patterns that repeated the great order of the created world endlessly. These myths might be called "mythopoetry," and they functioned with a "cloak of authority," for they were "the universal facts of life to which man must adjust himself."[26] Security was obtained by fitting into the divine harmony of the natural forces which interacted in the cosmos. Religious literature provided the key to that greatest good—"to be caught up within this cosmic rhythm of nature."[27]

Israel, however, saw the linear perspective of history beckon to an open road for human existence. Events did not repeat; therefore, life was not pre-determined. Great myths did not describe an endless pattern of cosmic reality. Myths, such as are found in Genesis 1–11, which spoke of a primordial divine-human experience that determined the nature of later social institutions, were transformed into epic material. For these primordial stories really spoke of non-repeatable experiences of the ancestors in a temporal sequence of events. Myth was broken and turned into epic by Israel's "historiographers." The past did not repeat, the future lay open, and no myth could chart the course of human existence. Epic offered only the hope of the continued relationship with the divine which had been experienced once, but not the ability to predict the future. For this reason divination would be disavowed in Israel. With the rise of epic as a normative form of religious expres-

14

sion the emphasis came to reside on human freedom and the corresponding responsibility it entails.[28]

With integration into the cosmic flux as an important goal for ancient Near Eastern people, their ritual and sacrifice assumed supreme importance. Cult offered a way of being initiated into the harmony of the cosmos and obtaining contact with the gods. Because the gods were felt to be akin to people, they would respond to prayers and gifts. Ritual was a mode of manipulating the gods, and festivals could be occasions wherein people engaged in rites of sympathetic magic to assume the identities of the various deities, act out a divine-human drama, and thus secure blessings and security in the natural realm. Fertility rites with a strong emphasis upon sexual activity as a mode of obtaining sympathetic harmony with the divine realm typified cultic behavior.[29]

Israel condemned divination and sympathetic magic officially (though they were tempted to practice it on a popular level), for one could not manipulate a deity who was transcendent over natural forces. Yahweh was not seen as a sexually active god with a female consort; there was no dying and rising god cult; and sexual activity for the sake of fertility was banned. Festivals were reinterpreted to highlight historical memories rather than eternal cosmic dramas; the saving acts of Yahweh in the past were seen as paradigmatic for future events. This paradigmatic view, however, was not the same as the cosmic repetitions in the rest of the ancient Near East according to the biblical theologians.[30]

Ancient Near Eastern society sought integration into the cosmic flux, security, and stability. This created a religion which endorsed the social-political status quo in society, a political-economic-ecclesiastical system. The goal was to "preserve the established order, and the whole cultic and social life" in order to maintain essential cosmic harmony. This static society would not tolerate any social reform, or a revolution for the sake of social justice.[31] Even Akhnaton's Egypt had "little sense of history or of social justice according to Biblical standards."[32] Generally ancient Near Eastern reli-

15

gions were responsible for the creation of socially oppressive societies.

In Israel the faith did not endorse a status quo in the political and economic realm but was to reform and occasionally encourage reform movements of major significance (Jehu's revolt, Hezekiah's reform, and the Deuteronomic reform under Josiah). "Dynamic change and revolution are to be expected because God is a dynamic being, external to the processes of life" and nature, directing history for the sake of His people.[33] This produced a dynamic view of the state in which the law guaranteed the equality of everyone, and the poor and defenseless received special consideration.[34]

The contrast between Israel and the nations manifested itself in the understanding of kingship. Kings in the ancient Near East were absolute, seen as divine and/or representatives of the gods, who advocated the changeless status quo and demanded the sacrifice of freedom for social stability and the integration of society and nature.[35]

Israelite kingship, however, was introduced by human initiative during the Philistine crisis despite divine and prophetic reservations. Since the institution arose within the relatively recent era according to the popular collective memory of the people, it could not be viewed as some divinely sent, pre-existent institution which undergirded the great cosmic fabric. Israelites could recall its creation and the accompanying controversy in their early historical experience. Kings were no closer to God than were the people, and these rulers were subservient to the will and laws of God, which occasionally were brought to bear by the excoriations of prophets. The sinfulness of kings would be publically condemned by the prophets, and finally the Deuteronomistic Historians would attribute the downfall of the nation in part to the folly of kings.[36]

In terms of morality ancient Near Eastern people, especially Mesopotamians, knew they were under a divine imperative, but they had no concept of law, therefore they lacked the sense that this imperative mandated social justice. Having no

16

consciousness of law, covenant, or election, but only a sense of subjection to destiny and the decrees of the gods, they could not equate individual laws with a greater concept of justice. Worshippers might confess sins but they lacked an ethical sense of guilt; they would regret but not repent. The individual was embedded in society, which in turn was embedded in the cosmic rhythms of nature. People were bound or determined by these forces, so that moral options were not available, and morality could not arise as an intellectual option. Israelites were bound together with Yahweh, who was the creator of nature and thus free from the cosmic forces. Likewise, people were free, capable of choosing their future course of action in moral and social categories. Freedom entails responsibility for actions, and with that comes the birth of morality and ethics, as we know it. Life was perceived not in terms of nature and security but in the light of divine will and the corresponding alignment of human will with divine will.[37]

After making these strident comparisons Wright could refer to Israel's worldview as a "breakthrough," or an "epigenesis," a "radical revolution" as opposed to simple evolution. This breakthrough was inexplicable according to the empirical data at our disposal. Perhaps Wright implied that this breakthrough might constitute some apologetic proof or testimony to the presence of divine activity in the life of ancient Israel. If so, Wright had a serious theological agenda for consideration by Christian theologians. Wright concluded:

> Thus it came about that the Biblical sense of history was born. The contemporary polytheisms, having analysed the problem of life over against nature, had little sense of or concern with the significance of history. Nature with its changing seasons was cyclical, and human life, constantly integrating itself with nature by means of cultic activity and sympathetic magic, moved with nature in a cyclical manner. But Israel was little interested in nature, except as God used it together with his historical acts to reveal himself and to accomplish his purpose. Yahweh was the God of history, the living god unaffected by the cycles of nature, who had set himself to accomplish a definite purpose in time.

17

Consequently, the religious literature of Israel was primarily concerned with the history of God's acts in and through his Chosen People. The great confessions of faith were primarily historical reviews of what God had done and what the people had done in response.[38]

D. Conclusion

Biblical theologians offered this model to students of religion: Israel was unique and stood in stark contrast to the values of the ancient Near East with its many deities acting in the phenomena of nature and the ever recurring cycles of the seasons, both symbolized mythically in the timeless action of cult. Dichotomies were clearly established: Israel was monotheistic, the ancient Near East was polytheistic; Israel had a linear or historical perspective on reality, the ancient Near East was cyclic or nature oriented; Israel emphasized human freedom and responsibility in this open-ended historical process, the ancient world stressed the pre-determined cosmic structures which fixed human fate in the cyclic pattern; Israel stressed law, ethics, and morality as the corollary of human freedom, while their contemporaries used sacrifice, cult, and ritual to bend or influence the cosmic pattern; Israel emphasized the religious and social equality of all its members, while in the ancient Near East oppression and slavery were permitted in society and in the religious cult human degradation with licentious sexual practices were found; and Israel articulated its beliefs in epics, the literature of the linear perspective, while in the ancient Near East cyclic oriented myths reflected the thought processes.

Israel was perceived as breaking radically with the ancient cultures that preceded it. Israel's monotheistic faith was in large part responsible for this departure from accepted thought patterns, and the clearest expression was found in the literature of "salvation history." Israel's unique contribution was this radical new worldview which would become the basis for later western culture.

Notes

1. Wright, "How did Early Israel differ from her Neighbors," *Biblical Archaeologist* 6 (1943): 1–10, 13–20, *God Who Acts, op. cit.,* pp. 11–128, and "Reflections concerning Old Testament theology," *Studia Biblica et Semitica,* eds. W. C. van Unnik and A. S. van der Woude (Wageningen: Veenman en Zonen, 1966), pp. 376–388, whose avowed agenda was to remove Scripture from a perception which viewed it in a systematic-theological way in order to understand it in its own historical and cultural context, while at the same time retaining the sense of unity between the Old and New Testaments. Millar Burrows, "Ancient Israel," *The Idea of History in the Ancient Near East,* ed. Robert Dentan, American Oriental Series, vol. 38 (New Haven: American Oriental Society, 1955), p. 128, voiced the strong theological conviction that in the arena of biblical history "our eternal, living God is working out his own sovereign purpose for the good of his creatures."

2. Wright, *The Old Testament Against Its Environment,* Studies in Biblical Theology, vol. 2 (Chicago: Regnery, 1950), pp. 7–112, *God Who Acts, op. cit.,* pp. 11–242, and Wright and Fuller, *Acts of God, op. cit.,* pp. 15–38; Oscar Cullmann, *Christ and Time: The Primitive Christian Conception of Time and History,* trans. Floyd Filson (Philadelphia: Westminster, 1950), pp. 11–242, who would state that "all Christian theology in its innermost essence is biblical history," p. 23; Burrows, "Ancient Israel," *op. cit.,* pp. 101–130; and Herbert Butterfield, *The Origins of History* (New York: Basic Books, 1981), pp. 80–117, who relied heavily upon the constructions of Gerhard von Rad, Martin Noth, and Albrecht Alt.

3. Cuthbert Simpson, "Old Testament Historiography and Revelation," *Hibbert Journal* (1957/1958): 319–332, and "An Inquiry into the Biblical Theology of History," *Journal of Theological Studies* 12 (1961): 1–13; and Gerhard von Rad, "Typological Interpretation of the Old Testament," trans. John Bright, *Essays on Old Testament Hermeneutics,* ed. Claus Westermann (Atlanta: John Knox, 1963), pp. 17–39. Reventlow, *Problems, op. cit.,* pp. 87–91, provided an extensive bibliography for the "Salvation History" discussion.

4. Martin Noth, "The Understanding of History in Old Testament Apocalyptic," *The Laws in the Pentateuch and other Studies,* trans. Dafydd Ap-Thomas (Philadelphia: Fortress, 1967), p. 195. However, in his later study of Mari prophecy, "History and Word of God in the Old Testament," *Laws, op. cit.,* p. 189, Noth was led to more

cautiously admit that the "qualitative difference between the Old Testament and its historical environment is removed."

5. Georg Fohrer, *History of Israelite Religion,* trans. David Green (Nashville: Abingdon, 1972), p. 182.

6. Sigmund Mowinckel, *He That Cometh,* trans. George Anderson (Oxford, England: Blackwell, 1956), p. 151. Cf. his article, "Israelite Historiography," *Annual of the Swedish Theological Institute* 2 (1963): 4–26.

7. Theodore Vriezen, *An Outline of Old Testament Theology* (Oxford, England: Blackwell, 1958), p. 187.

8. Cullman, *Time, op. cit.,* p. 51.

9. Burrows, "Ancient Israel," *op. cit.,* p. 127.

10. Wright, *God Who Acts, op. cit.,* p. 24.

11. Butterfield, *History, op. cit.,* p. 88.

12. Alfred Jepsen, *Die Quellen des Königsbuches* (Halle: Niemeyer, 1956), p. 114; and Noth, "Geschichtsschreibung. I. Im Alten Testament," *Die Religion in Geschichte und Gegenwart,* 6 vols., 3rd ed., ed. Kurt Galling (Tübingen: Mohr, 1958), 2:1499–1500.

13. Walther Eichrodt, "Offenbarung und Geschichte im Alten Testament," *Theologische Zeitschrift* 4 (1948): 322, 329; and von Rad, "Theologische Geschichtsschreibung im Alten Testament," *Theologische Zeitschrift* 4 (1948): 161.

14. James Montgomery, *A Critical and Exegetical Commentary on the Books of Kings,* ed. Henry Gehman, International Critical Commentary (New York: Scribner's, 1951), pp. 25–30; Jepsen, *Quellen, op. cit.,* pp. 106–114; Noth, "Geschichtsschreibung," *op. cit.,* pp. 1498–1499; Johannes Lindblom, *Prophecy in Ancient Israel* (London: Blackwell, 1962), p. 325; and Butterfield, *History, op. cit.,* p. 98.

15. Burr Brundage, "The Birth of Clio: A Resume and Interpretation of Ancient Near Eastern Historiography," *Teachers of History: Essays in Honor of Laurence Bradford Packard,* ed. Stuart Hughes (Ithaca: Cornell University, 1954), p. 200.

16. Wright, *God Who Acts, op. cit.,* pp. 38–39; Ludlow Bull, "Ancient Egypt," *Idea of History, op. cit.,* pp. 21–22, 32–33; Ephraim Speiser, "Ancient Mesopotamia," *Idea of History, op. cit.,* pp. 55, 67; and Butterfield, *History, op. cit.,* p. 98.

17. Noth, "Von der Knechtgestalt des Alten Testaments," *Evangelische Theologie* 6 (1946/1947): 305; and Hans Wildberger, "Auf dem Wege zu einer biblischen Theologie," *Evangelische Theologie* 19 (1959): 77.

18. Jepsen, *Quellen, op. cit.*, p. 106.

19. Mowinckel, "Historiography," *op. cit.*, p. 8.

20. Butterfield, *History, op. cit.*, pp. 80–81.

21. Lindblom, *Prophecy, op. cit.*, p. 326.

22. *Ibid.*, p. 325.

23. Wright, "Early Israel," *op. cit.*, pp. 1–10, 13–20, and "Reflections," *op. cit.*, pp. 376-388; Noth, "Knechtgestalt," *op. cit.*, p. 307, pointed out that Augustine transmitted linear categories of Israelite thought to the west; Eric Voegelin, *Order and History*, vol. 1: *Israel and Revelation* (Baton Rouge: Louisiana State University, 1956), pp. 1–515, evaluated history and intellectual development as an attempt to bring order to reality, and Israel used linear categories to order their perception of reality; Friedrich Baumgärtel, "Das Offenbarungszeugnis des Alten Testaments im Lichte der religionsgeschichtlich-vergleichenden Forschung," *Zeitschrift für Theologie und Kirche* 64 (1967): 393–422; Butterfield, *History, op. cit.*, pp. 86–87; Irving Zeitlin, *Ancient Judaism* (Cambridge, England: Polity, 1984), pp. 1–35; and Bernhard Anderson, *Understanding the Old Testament*, 4th ed. (Englewood Cliffs, New Jersey: Prentice-Hall, 1986), pp. 184–193, still used these categories in the latest edition of his introduction.

24. Wright, "Early Israel," *op. cit.*, pp. 7–8, *Old Testament, op. cit.*, p. 17, and *Acts of God., op cit.*, p. 30; and Zeitlin, *Judaism, op. cit.*, pp. 28, 33. Cf. Mircea Eliade, *The Myth of the Eternal Return or, Cosmos and History*, trans. Willard Trask, Bollingen Series, vol. 46 (Princeton: Princeton University, 1954), pp. 3–162, described this view quite well; and Thorkild Jacobsen, *The Treasures of Darkness: A History of Mesopotamian Religion* (New Haven: Yale University, 1976), pp. 23–73, described early Mesopotamian religion of the fourth millennium B.C. in a way which corresponds to this; albeit, his description of subsequent Mesopotamian religion differed significantly with this portrayal.

25. Wright, "Early Israel," *op. cit.*, pp. 7–8, and *Old Testament, op. cit.*, p. 23: Jepsen, *Quellen, op. cit.*, p. 114; and Baumgärtel, "Offenbarungszeugnis," *op. cit.*, pp. 393–422.

26. Wright, *Old Testament, op. cit.*, p. 19. Cf. Wright, "Early Israel," *op. cit.*, pp. 7–8; and Zeitlin, *Judaism, op. cit.*, p. 21.

27. Wright, *God Who Acts, op. cit.*, p. 39.

28. Wright, "Early Israel," *op. cit.*, pp. 7–8; Speiser, "The Biblical Idea of History in its Common Near Eastern Setting," *Israel Exploration Journal* 7 (1957): 201–216; and Zeitlin, *Judaism, op. cit.*, p. 21.

29. Wright, *Old Testament, op. cit.*, p. 102, *God Who Acts, op. cit.*, p. 28; and Zeitlin, *Judaism, op. cit.*, pp. 30–33.

30. Wright, *Old Testament, op. cit.*, pp. 78–90, and *God Who Acts, op. cit.*, p. 28; Baumgärtel, "Offenbarungszeugnis," *op. cit.*, pp. 393–422; and Vriezen, *The Religion of Ancient Israel*, trans. H. Hoskins (Philadelphia: Westminster, 1967), p. 73.

31. Wright, *Old Testament, op. cit.*, pp. 44–45.

32. *Ibid.*, p. 38. Cf. James Henry Breasted, *The Dawn of Conscience* (New York: Scribner's, 1933), pp. 115–222, 272–420, who would disagree vehemently on this observation.

33. Wright, *God Who Acts, op. cit.*, p. 22.

34. Wright, *Old Testament, op. cit.*, p. 59, and *ibid.*, pp. 19–29, admitted this concern occurred elsewhere, but it lacked the emphasis found in Israel.

35. Wright, *Old Testament, op. cit.*, p. 63.

36. Henri Frankfort, *Kingship and the Gods: A Study of Ancient Near Eastern Religion as the Integration of Society and Nature* (Chicago: University of Chicago, 1948), pp. 339–344, offered one of the best comparisons of Israelite and ancient Near Eastern kingship models.

37. Wright, "Early Israel," *op. cit.*, pp. 16–17, *Old Testament, op. cit.*, pp. 69, 106, and *God Who Acts, op. cit.*, p. 20; and *ibid.*, p. 278.

38. Wright, *Old Testament, op. cit.*, p. 71.

Chapter 3
The Critical Theological Response

Within the last twenty five years this *Heilsgeschichte* model has been criticized in many ways. Brevard Childs has even spoken of the "death" of the greater Biblical Theology Movement which supported salvation history perceptions of the biblical text as one of their primary theological agenda.[1] Criticism has come from philosophical, theological, biblical, as well as from ancient Near Eastern scholarship. Though our purpose is to consider primarily the ancient Near Eastern relationship, it would be useful to give summary consideration to the general theological criticisms of the *Heilsgeschichte* model.

A. Theological Criticism

From a philosophical and theological perspective the notions of revelation and history which were used by biblical theologians were given critical scrutiny and found lacking in clarity. How can the Exodus and Resurrection be concrete events in history and revelatory events apprehended only by faith at the same time? There was confusion between salvation history accessible to critical study for the verification of particular biblical ideals and the salvation history grasped only by faith. Critics like James Barr asserted that biblical theologians could not have it both ways; if it is history, it can be studied, and then it is not revelation or an object of faith alone.[2]

Biblical theologians had not defined clearly the relationship between history and revelation to the satisfaction of systematic theologians. Is history itself revelation or just a special process in the historical continuum? Essentially both positions were found to be articulated among biblical theologians—a sign that the issue had never been clarified.[3] Barr suggested that biblical authors were inspired not by historical events which were recorded for us in the texts, but they were inspired and influenced far more by their perceptions of those events. The biblical text contains the subjective theological perceptions of biblical thinkers; we have their "thought patterns," their mode of interpreting events, rather than a direct testimony of the events. Scriptures contain not a theology of salvation history but a theology of Israel's religious perspective, their way of thinking, as the foundation for our biblical theology.[4]

The biblical text is theological explications or meditations on historical events. There are no bare accounts of divine action without an interpretation—we have revelation through verbal communication which interprets actions.[5] Barr stated it well:

> A God who acted in history would be a mysterious and supra-personal fate if the action was not linked with this verbal conversation. . . . In his speech with man, . . . God really meets man on his own level and directly.[6]

God communicates verbally, the historical setting is merely a foil, or a trivial variable, according to Barr. Actions are linked together and interpreted by speeches and divine communication. The Scriptures contain revelation about history not revelation in history; Word not Act describes the nature of the biblical text and its revelation most clearly.[7]

The relation between events and the texts which narrate them was left unexplained by biblical theologians. How can a revelation in history be communicated through a written text? How can historical events be central when they are recorded in narrative material which does not emphasize historicity as we understand it? The mere fact that we must use literary texts in constructing a theology of history undermines the entire process, for we work with literary materials as the primary source not history. We have a theology built upon texts which reflect upon historical events.

The Hebrew Scriptures do not have a notion or even a word for the term history, rather we have impressed it upon the text. The distinction between *Heilsgeschichte* and *Weltgeschichte*, or *Geschichte* and *Historie* are our own artificial constructions.[8] J. J. M. Roberts pointed out that biblical scholars too often moved beyond a literary category of history (which is historiography) to a philosophical category of history, which entailed human freedom and developed eschatology, and then they attributed this to the biblical tradition. Even modern positivistic historical methods do not assume human free will or eschatological purpose, and therefore they would fail to meet the criteria of "history writing" as established by biblical theologians.[9] To define a notion of history from a modern confessional stance and then to attribute it to the biblical was hardly acceptable scholarly procedure. But perhaps biblical theologians had done this unconsciously in an effort to make the biblical texts speak relevantly to modern theological issues.

B. Exegetical Criticism

A second avenue of critique arose among biblical scholars themselves. From the biblical-exegetical perspective salvation history models were criticized because they disregarded the non-historical material in the biblical text, such as Wisdom Literature, Psalms, legal materials, and literature which emphasize that God is lord of the created order in general, not just the historical arena. These other literary genres imply that God acts in the total arena of human existence, and the biblical materials are designed to give full testimony to divine self-disclosure.[10]

Even the "historical" texts were perceived to be more like historiography than was actually the case. Most of the biblical narrative texts were really epic, legend, aetiological accounts, and even myths or semi-mythic tales, all of which should not be called "history" in the modern sense. Critics compared biblical material to Greek historiography and found that the biblical texts lacked key elements of an overall objectivity in the quest for truth, nor did they have factual and evaluative ways of dealing with individual accounts. True historical consciousness reflects itself in the use of words for truth (as evidenced in the Greek historians), but in Hebrew the words for truth are subjective words which imply faithfulness in belief. The Hebrew Scriptures lacked a notion of individual consciousness as found among the Greeks, hence any distanced, objective historiography could not have been written. "Historical" texts in the Hebrew Canon were connected to matters of faith and uninterested in reported events as the record of general human accomplishments (as in Herodotus).[11]

Narrative in the Hebrew Scriptures actually had closer connections with the literature of the ancient Near East in terms of historiographical approach. While biblical theologians emphasized Israel's historical and linear perspective, some biblical texts reflected the cyclic view of the ancient Near East quite strongly. The Primeval History of the Yahwist Epic account in Genesis 2–11 and the Deuteronomistic History (Joshua through Kings) perceived cycles of sin, punishment, and forgiveness in human events. Scholars like John Curtis isolated evidence of cyclic thought in other biblical texts, including the book of Koheleth, the Israelite festival cycle, Deutero-Isaiah's view of creation-exodus-return from exile, Hosea's call to return to the wilderness for renewed faithfulness to Yahweh, and the general hope for a Davidic age in the future. Biblical theologians did not view this material as cyclic, mythic, or non-historical; but they quickly discerned such cyclic patterns in similar ancient Near Eastern materials.[12]

Biblical theologians had taken pre-critical language of the Israelites and unconsciously modernized it with their own religious values. Israelite discourse and imagery of divine action in human affairs were transformed into the modern concept of history, and their description of individual accounts was sometimes filtered by commentators to sound like a modern historical rendition.[13] As a result it has become increasingly common among theological and exegetical critics to speak more of the biblical texts as story narrative rather than history, so as to avoid the category mistake of forcing the modern concept of history upon proto-historical or pre-critical texts.[14]

Thus from a biblical perspective salvation history models were criticized for being an inadequate theological expression to use in discussing biblical materials. Salvation history models ignored much of the text and subjectively nuanced other portions of the biblical text to be viewed as more historical than they really were.[15]

C. Criticism of Ancient Near Eastern Scholars

The third avenue of critique arose among ancient Near Eastern scholars who were offended by the unfair generalizations made about the culture and values of the societies contemporary with Israel. It is their critique with which we shall be more interested in this work and in the ensuing chapters, but at this point some general observations ought to be noted.

These scholars disdained the denigration of ancient Near Eastern thought for the sake of affirming Israel's intellectual and theological uniqueness. Their responses addressed several issues: 1) Israel was not totally distinct in monotheistic tendencies; several movements in Egypt and Mesopotamia elevated a universal high god during the first and second millenniums B.C.[16] 2) Nor did Israel have a monopoly on social justice. Social reformers who sensed the rights of poor and oppressed arose in Egypt and Mesopotamia.[17] 3) Notions concerning the encounter with the divine, creation, good and evil, and universalism were not diametrically opposed but were actually more continuous between the ancient Near East and Israel.[18] 4) The notion of gods acting in the realm of history and political affairs was found among Hittites and Assyrians as well as in Israel.[19] And 5) the historiographical literary form may be found among the Hittites and Assyrians; Israel did not invent it but inherited it.[20] One is reminded of how Albrecht Alt once claimed apodictic law to be Israel's unique contribution to intellectual development, then parallel apodictic forms were discovered in ancient Near Eastern literature and lawcodes. The message of these critics was that we should not try to distinguish too radically between Israelite and ancient Near Eastern thought, especially in terms of historical consciousness.[21]

In our consideration of the critique provided by ancient Near Eastern scholars there are three works worthy of notice: 1) Bertil Albrektson, *History and the Gods*, 1967, produced the pivotal critique around which the debate has raged in his discussion of salvation history models in Israel and Mesopotamia. 2) H. W. F. Saggs, *The Encounter with the Divine in Mesopotamia and Israel*, 1978, provided a more general discussion of several areas of religious values, showing the great similarities between Israel and Mesopotamia. And 3) John Van Seters, *In Search of History*, 1983, described the historiographical materials of Egyptians, Mesopotamians, Hittites, Canaanites, and Israelites in thorough fashion. All three works criticized the facile comparisons made between Israel and the ancient world.

In general ancient historians accused biblical scholars of being simplistic in their evaluation. Saggs and others critiqued them for not applying the same criteria in equal measure to biblical and ancient Near Eastern texts; biblical scholars made a theological evaluation of the biblical texts, but a phenomenological evaluation of ancient Near Eastern texts. The Hebrew Scriptures were assessed according to the theological perspective of the final form of the canon, which had been subjected to the critical redaction of exilic and post-exilic monotheists with their high moral values. Ancient Near Eastern texts drawn from the ground by archaeology represented an unfiltered version of the actual religious beliefs and customs ranging from popular superstitious practice to sophisticated religious reflection. Such comparison naturally viewed the ancient Near Eastern material pejoratively.[22] J. J. M. Roberts pointed out the tendency of biblical scholars to make comparisons with earlier and more primitive Mesopotamian religion to highlight differences. The early Mesopotamian religion sought "integration into the forces of nature" in order to manipulate them and this indeed contrasted with the later Israelite cultic understandings which stressed "adjustment to the will of God." But early Israelite views of the cult paralleled Mesopotamian counterparts, and likewise Mesopotamian cultic understandings in the later period were more sophisticated.[23] Mesopotamian religion moved from early "sympathetic magic for the sake of fertility to later anthropomorphic and sociomorphic forms for social and psychological needs in the community," according to Thorkild Jacobsen and Roberts.[24] George Ernest Wright was criticized in particular for choosing the earlier Mesopotamian world in order "to paint a sharp contrast between the pagan . . . and the Israelite," between sympathetic magic and adjustment to divine will.[25] Biblical theologians had an agenda for the contemporary world and they were willing to skew their assessment of the ancient Near East. Biblical theologians wished to declare Israel unique among the nations, and Bertil Albrektson referred to a truly revealing quote by Sigmund Mowinckel making this very observation:

> If historical events as a medium of revelation is a general Near Eastern conception and the limited content of a revelation conveyed through this medium is conceived in much the same way both by the Israelites and by their neighbors, then there is very little foundation indeed for the common claim to distinctiveness on this particular point.[26]

Critics of the biblical theologians would declare that Mowinckel had uncovered the most sensitive nerve of the salvation history model and its proponents. Roberts would admit that there is some truth in the contrast between the historical and free-will orientation of Israel and the a-historical and manipulative perspective of the ancient Near East, but there are "weaknesses in the analysis" which are found not only in popular presentations, but they "are not totally absent from the more sophisticated treatments."[27]

D. Conclusion

Criticisms were brought against the salvation history models from several directions. Theologically the model was criticized for the lack of clarity concerning the relationship of divine activity and human history. Exegetically the model was found lacking in its failure to honestly portray the material in the biblical text. Finally, ancient Near Eastern scholars declared that the model either ignored or pejoratively evaluated the comparative literature of the ancient world.

The goal of this study shall focus upon the last consideration in greater detail. Understanding the "historical" or "narrative" literature of the Hebrew Scriptures within the contemporary cultural context of that age might lead us to a more precise understanding of what it means to call this material "salvation history" and what religious and cultural implications developed from it.

Notes

1. Brevard Childs, *Biblical Theology in Crisis* (Philadelphia: Westminster, 1970), pp. 13–87. Cf. Morton Smith, "The Present State of Old Testament Studies," *Journal of Biblical Literature* 88 (1969): 19–35; and James Barr, *Biblical Words for Time*, Studies in Biblical Theology, vol. 33 (Naperville, Illinois: Allenson, 1962), pp. 11–162, and *Old and New in Interpretation: A Study of the Two Testaments* (London: SCM, 1982), pp. 34–64, assaulted the simplistic distinctions between Hebraic or biblical thought and the Greek or pagan world; this too, was one of the major perceptions of the Biblical Theology Movement. Reventlow, *Problems, op. cit*, pp. 59–124, offered the best bibliography and a terse summary of this debate.

2. Barr, "The Problem of Old Testament Theology and the History of Religion," *Canadian Journal of Theology* 3 (1957): 141–149, "The Interpretation of Scripture: II. Revelation Through History in the Old

Testament and in Modern Theology," *Interpretation* 17 (1963): 198, and *Old and New, op. cit.*, pp. 66–69; and Alberto Soggin, "Geschichte, Historie and Heilsgeschichte im Alten Testament," *Theologische Literaturzeitung* 89 (1964): 721–736.

3. Franz Hesse, "Bewährt sich eine 'Theologie der Heilstatsachen' im Alten Testament?," *Zeitschrift für die alttestamentliche Wissenschaft* 81 (1969): 1–18.

4. Barr, "Revelation in History," *Interpreter's Dictionary of the Bible, Supplement*, ed. Keith Crim (Nashville: Abingdon, 1976), p. 747.

5. Barr, "Interpretation," *op. cit.*, p. 197, and *Old and New, op. cit.*, p. 19; and Bertil Albrektson, *History and the Gods: An Essay on the Idea of Historical Events as Divine Manifestations in the Ancient Near East and in Israel* (Lund: Gleerup, 1967), p. 120.

6. Barr, *Old and New, op. cit.*, p. 78.

7. Barr, "Revelation," *op. cit.*, p. 747, and *ibid.*, pp. 15–33, 77–82; and Albrektson, *History, op. cit.*, pp. 119–122.

8. Barr, "Interpretation," *op. cit.*, p. 199; and Rudolf Smend, *Elemente alttestamentlichen Geschichtsdenkens*, Theologische Studien, vol. 95 (Zurich: EVZ, 1968), p. 36.

9. J. J. M. Roberts, "Myth versus History: Relaying the Comparative Foundations," *Catholic Biblical Quarterly* 38 (1976): 3–4.

10. Roland Murphy, "Wisdom and Yahwism," *No Famine in the Land: Studies in honor of John L. McKenzie*, eds. James Flanagan and Anita Robinson (Missoula, Montana: Scholars Press, 1975), pp. 119–120; and Barr, *Old and New, op. cit.*, pp. 15–33, 72–76.

11. Smend, *Elemente, op. cit.*, pp. 3–37; and Hubert Cancik, *Mythische und historische Wahrheit: Interpretationen zu Texten der hethitischen, biblischen und griechischen Historiographie*, Stuttgarter Bibelstudien, vol. 48 (Stuttgart: Katholisches Bibelwerk, 1970), pp. 91–108.

12. John Briggs Curtis, "A Suggested Interpretation of the Biblical Philosophy of History," *Hebrew Union College Annual* 34 (1963): 115–123. Erich Dinkler, "Earliest Christianity," *Idea of History, op. cit.*, pp. 181–191, even discerned cyclic thought in the writings of Paul.

13. Barr, "Problem," *op. cit.*, pp. 141–149; and Langdon Gilkey, "Cosmology, Ontology, and the Travail of Biblical Language," *Journal of Religion* 41 (1961): 194–205.

14. Thorleif Boman, *Hebrew Thought Compared with Greek*,

trans. Jules Moreau (London: SCM, 1960), pp. 1–17; and Lindblom, *Prophecy, op. cit.*, pp. 748–749.

15. Barr, "Interpretation," *op. cit.*, pp. 193–205, and *Old and New, op. cit.*, pp. 65–102.

16. See the essays in Othmar Keel, ed., *Monotheismus im Alten Israel und seiner Umwelt*, Biblische Beiträge, vol. 14 (Stuttgart: Katholische Bibelwerk, 1980), pp. 12–184.

17. Breasted, *Dawn, op. cit.*, pp. 272–335; and Charles Fensham, "Widow, Orphan, and the Poor in Ancient Near Eastern Legal and Wisdom Literature," *Journal of Near Eastern Studies* 21 (1962): 129–139.

18. H. W. F. Saggs, *The Encounter with the Divine in Mesopotamia and Israel*, Jordan Lectures in Comparative Religion, vol. 12 (London: Athlone, 1978), pp. 1–224.

19. Albrektson, *History, op. cit.*, pp. 11–122; and Saggs, *Encounter, op. cit.*, pp. 64–92.

20. John Van Seters, *In Search of History: Historiography in the Ancient World and the Origins of Biblical History* (New Haven: Yale University, 1983), pp. 209–248.

21. Lindblom, *Prophecy, op. cit.*, p. 325; Wilfrid Lambert, "History and the Gods: A Review Article," *Orientalia* 39 (1970): 171–172; Roberts, "Myth Versus History," *op. cit.*, p. 12; Saggs, *Encounter, op. cit.*, pp. 4, 90–92; Butterfield, *History, op. cit.*, p. 86; Barr *Old and New, op. cit.*, pp. 71–72; and *ibid.*, pp. 360–361.

22. Claus Westermann, "Sinn und Grenze religionsgeschichtlicher Parallelen," *Theologische Literaturzeitung* 90 (1965): 489–496; and Saggs, *Encounter, op. cit.*, pp. 1–29 et passim.

23. Roberts, "Divine Freedom and Cultic Manipulation in Israel and Mesopotamia," *Unity and Diversity: Essays in the History, Literature, and Religion of the Ancient Near East*, eds. Hans Goedicke and Roberts (Baltimore: Johns Hopkins University, 1975), pp. 182–183.

24. Jacobsen, "Religious Drama in Ancient Mesopotamia," *Unity and Diversity, op. cit.*, pp. 65–77; and *ibid.*, p. 183.

25. Roberts, "Cultic Manipulation," *op. cit.*, p. 183.

26. Mowinckel, "Historiography," *op. cit.*, p. 8, which was commented upon by Albrektson, *History, op. cit.*, p. 114.

27. Roberts, "Cultic Manipulation," *op. cit.*, p. 181.

Chapter 4
Ancient Near Eastern and Biblical Historiography

Ancient Near Eastern scholars responded to biblical theologians to defend the integrity of ancient thought and to minimize the contrasts presented by the salvation history paradigm. The central issue was the question of historiographical materials, and the capacity of the ancient Near Eastern peoples to produce such literature. Other issues concerning the differences of similarities in matters of revelation, religious belief, and cultic practice seemed to be dependent upon the historiographical question. Scholars were quick to point out that the ancient world produced material quite comparable to that found in Israel. Thus we turn our attention to this issue for particular consideration.

A. Value of Ancient Near Eastern Historiographical Literature

Historians affirmed the ability of the ancient Near Eastern thinkers to produce documents worthy to be called historiography. Special attention was paid to the accomplishments of Mesopotamians, especially the writings of the Assyrians, who were contemporary with Israel. A few specialists also highlighted Hittite documents as worthy of consideration and respect for being the most advanced form of historiography in the ancient Near East.

Ancient Near Eastern scholars chided biblical theologians

on several issues. Biblical scholars too often ignored pertinent ancient materials or dismissed them with minimal consideration.[1] Among biblical theologians the common assumption was that true historiography arose out of epic literature and not inscriptions or annals, and therewith the epic literature offered itself as the primary candidate for the origin of history writing.[2] Scholars like John Van Seters and others responded with evidence that historiography more properly arose out of the annalistic tradition, as was the case with the Greek historians.[3] If so, then the military reports and the entire annalistic tradition of the Egyptians, Hittites, and Assyrians provided fertile ground for the rise of historiography. Other scholars maintained that the earlier and more basic building inscriptions of the Mesopotamians laid the foundation. Historiography may be seen to evolve out of early lists, such as the Sumerian King List and other chronicles and annals.[4]

The stereotype of an ancient Near Eastern cyclic worldview was denied. The culture in Mesopotamia developed a noncyclic view of reality at least by the second millennium B.C. which would have the ability to interpret events from a particular viewpoint, observe how they developed, and perceive how they led up to the present time. Such a worldview was most responsible for producing the Hittite and Assyrian historiographical materials.[5] Several scholars proposed that history writing might have firm roots even in the third millennium B.C. with the "chancery style" of the Sumerians, Mesopotamian building inscriptions, and Sumerian King List (which observes the times before the flood were quite different than the present—implying some change and development).[6] Perhaps undiscovered sources might be found to further verify this opinion. Hayim Tadmor implied that were we to have more resources, our respect of the ancient Near East would be much higher. He suspected that Assyrian and Hittite annals might be dependent upon even earlier Amorite models in the early second millennium B.C.[7]

Biblical theologians were unaccustomed to identify historiography in its ancient Near Eastern context. For example,

Mesopotamian historiography appears to be connected with divination at times, and therefore was rejected as true history by modern biblical scholars. Nevertheless, Mesopotamians looked to the exemplary nature of events. This is the same reason modern people study history. For the ancients believed that if under certain circumstances an event might be repeated, then past events merit consideration, so as to prepare for the future. Essentially this is the purpose behind modern study of history; we seek the paradigm in order to approximate the possible outcome of contemporary events.[8] Ancient people simply used less variables in their consideration, and some of these "variables" (signs and portents) would simply be discarded by modern historians in favor of other factors.

The mode of perceiving past events in the ancient Near East was not altogether unlike that found in Israel. Ancient people perceived historical flow in the successive rise and decline of political dynasties. This "rhythmic regularity" was "suggestive of cosmic laws" upon which one could build a view of history. Furthermore, the disruption of successive political regimes was explained by the motif of the anger of the gods; "theological offense as grounds for historic change" was the basic presupposition of the ancient materials. This notion is the same as that found in the Deuteronomistic History—obedience or disobedience to the will of Yahweh and his laws would bring either blessing or punishment in the course of human events.[9]

Biblical scholars too often moved beyond a literary category of historiography, which ancient Near Eastern scholars used in their consideration of the texts, to a special philosophical category of history inherited from the Christian tradition. This special philosophical category entailed the potential of humans to act with a free will in determining their future and an ultimate culmination to history which would appropriately reward or punish those decisions (eschatology). Both aspects of human free will and eschatology are usually lacking in modern forms of historiography, especially secular, empirical, positivistic history.[10] With their narrow definition of historiography biblical scholars were naturally inclined to exclude ancient Near Eastern materials unfairly.

Likewise biblical scholars were often critical of the literary quality of the ancient Near Eastern sources, calling them merely lists or annals. These materials were said to be placed together in a non-systematic fashion or piecemeal as uneven sources. Yet J. J. M. Roberts and others would point out by way of response that biblical scholars had described Penta-teuchal and Deuteronomistic materials as uneven sources woven together in not always consistent fashion. If we criticize the ancient Near Eastern historians for placing disparate blocks of pre-existing literature in conjunction with each other, we must be ready to admit that this was also the method undertaken by the Deuteronomistic Historians with many of their pre-literary and simple literary sources.[11]

Consistently biblical theologians failed to acknowledge the quality of ancient Near Eastern materials. They were ready to denigrate them in favor of biblical materials without recognizing the same critical observations might be made of the biblical texts.

B. Mesopotamian Sources

Many examples of annalistic literature can be evaluated as having historiographical value according to ancient Near Eastern specialists. Special attention can be given to Babylonian and Assyrian sources, and the following are some of the significant works isolated for consideration by ancient historians.

Among the Babylonians a number of documents were produced which merit the description of historical chronicle. One of the earliest appears to be the Curse of Akkad, an account explaining the reason for the collapse of the Akkadian Empire in the late third millennium B.C. The oldest copy comes from Nippur in south Mesopotamia from around 2050 B.C. The chronicle describes how the gods punish people in the course of human history.[12] Though some critics have referred to it as a hymnic lamentation, Samuel Kramer and Bertil Albrektson prefer to describe it as a "historiographic document written in highly poetic prose" rather than a lamentation.[13] Kramer considers it "one of the earliest recorded attempts to interpret a historical event in the framework of a currently held world view."[14] Overall, the early nature of the material allows for a certain disagreement concerning its historiographical quality.

Later Babylonian documents, however, developed a clearer historiographical quality under the auspices of the priests of Marduk. According to Burr Brundage the period between the Old Babylonian and the Neo-Babylonian eras (1800–550 B.C.) saw the development of history writing move in a secular direction—the gods were seen to be no longer absolutely necessary. Written history freed itself to become a literary discipline "humanistic at its center though still leaving wide peripheral areas for divine and providential intervention."[15] Though the gods were active in human affairs, Brundage sensed that the real cause and motivation for human history was in human actions. Several scholars have also noted that the alternation between periods of order and chaos occurs in these texts in a fashion comparable to that found in the Deuteronomistic History.[16] Though not all scholars would agree with these assessments, nonetheless there appears to be a qualitative advance in the historiographical literature.

The most well known work from this period is the Weidner Chronicle, a document describing the fall of various Mesopotamian dynasties from early Sumer through the Third Dynasty of Ur (3000–2000 B.C.). Scholars like Eva Osswald have seen striking parallels between this document and the Deuteronomistic History, for the Weidner Chronicle attributes the fall of various cities and their rulers to the displeasure of the gods for human neglect of Marduk's cult and his divine authority.[17] Herein the connection between human action and consequence is evident, for the gods respond to direct events as a result of human behavior. One might speak of causality in history, a rather advanced notion appearing in early form.[18]

37

The work has been called a "milestone in the origins of historiography" and reflects the new intellectual vigor of the priests in service to the cult of Marduk and the political supremacy of Babylon.[19] Debate exists as to whether it belongs to the Amorite Babylonian Dynasty (early second millennium B.C.) or the later Kassite Babylonian period (late second millennium B.C.). Either way it represents a significant attempt to undergird existing religious and political institutions with an ideology justified by a highly interpreted overview of past political events. With such a religious-political orientation the document certainly compares to later literature considered to be historiographical; even modern "objective" history writing often interprets events from the perspective of a contemporary ideology.

Though not of the same significance, nevertheless worthy of consideration, are the accounts of the Kassite king, Nebuchadrezzar I (1125–1103 B.C.). These chronicles describe his return of the images of Marduk from Elam and are similar to Israelite interpretations of the Babylonian exile. According to the accounts Marduk left Babylon for exile in Elam because of his anger against his own people; he returned only because of his mercy. Throughout he is portrayed as having been in total control of human affairs both in Babylon and Elam.[20] The parallel with the Deuteronomistic History is again striking.

Assyrian historical sources from the reign of Adad-Nirari III (809–782 B.C.) trace significant events and accomplishments of the kings of Babylon and Assyria from the fifteenth century B.C. to the time of their composition. Though fragmentary in nature and of limited chronological value, their significance lies in the occasional correlation of events between Babylon and Assyria, which provides a basis for organizing information from other more thorough king lists. These Synchronistic Chronicles include the Synchronistic History and Chronicle P. Of special interest is the Synchronistic History, for it interprets the historial relationship between Assyria and Babylon from the perspective of conflict over land ownership. The unjust violations of boundary agreements by the Babylonians in the distant past and present warrant Assyrian vengeance. Thus the work interprets history with the purpose of justifying intended Assyrian actions. These Assyrian reports are highly propagandistic and very suspect in terms of their historical reliability.[21] Most interesting, however, is the correlation of the actions of Babylonian and Assyrian kings. The similarity with the Deuteronomistic History is obvious and invites the suggestion that Assyrian annals inspired the Israelite undertaking.

The latest work is the Babylonian Chronicle Series which contains fifteen various texts. The primary concern of most of the texts is Neo-Babylonian history from 747 to 539 B.C., hence the materials sometimes are called the Neo-Babylonian Chronicle. But other texts, including the Chronicle of the Early Kings, Chronicle P, and the Ecclectic Chronicle, trace events back to the time of Sargon of Akkad in the late third millennium B.C. Scholars have often commended the Babylonian Chronicle Series for the accuracy and objectivity found in the accounts. Close analogies again have been drawn with the Deuteronomistic History and especially the books of Kings.[22] Though the materials cover the same events as the Assyrian Synchronistic History, they are far more reliable in their representation of the historical events.[23] As was the case with the earlier Weidner Chronicle the entire Babylonian Chronicle Series views the sovereignty of Marduk as the central focus around which the events of humanity transpire. Most noteworthy is the length of time covered by the texts, nearly two millennia. Frequently biblical theologians had decried ancient Near Eastern sources as inadequate forms of historiography because they did not evaluate long periods of time as did the biblical authors. However, the Babylonian Chronicle Series overviews a time span four times that of the Deuteronomistic History.

Assyrian historiography may have been inspired by the earlier Hittite materials rather than Babylonian. These texts merit consideration even though they are said to lack the literary quality of the Babylonian Chronicle Series just discussed.[24] In addition to the Synchronistic History a number of reports and references in various texts merit our attention because of their value in relation to Israel's mode of discourse in the narrative and prophetic literature. H. W. F. Saggs believed that in the first millennium B.C. with the rise of the Assyrian Empire the cyclic world view was replaced by the historical perspective. Assyrians perceived themselves as agents of the deity Ashur commissioned to establish a universal religious-political kingdom, and the literature produced by this quest spoke of a divine plan in history. This permitted the change and innovation typical of that period to arise, and it created the specimens of Assyrian historiography which we possess.[25]

Since many of the references worthy of note occur in various texts, we cannot speak of a significant historiographical work. Thus we shall defer discussion of particular Assyrian examples until later when the discussion of major comparative themes requires reference to selected texts for exemplification.

Within the greater Mesopotamian cultural sphere should also be included the Syro-Palestinian region, the area of West-Semitic peoples. This literature has been discussed on occasion for its historiographical quality, especially Ugaritic and Aramean texts. The Keret Epic from Ugarit is said to exhibit as much historical consciousness as is found in the patriarchal narratives according to Nicolas Wyatt.[26] Likewise a number of Aramean inscriptions offer themselves for consideration: 1) the Zakir inscription, 2) the Melqart Stela of Ben-Hadad, 3) several of the Sefire treaties, and 4) the Panammu and Berrakab inscriptions. Wyatt believed these materials display the same level of historical consciousness as the Hebrew Scriptures in general.[27] Most significantly the Moabite Mesha stone provides a stunning parallel to "the Israelite idea of divine rule and a divine revelation in historical events."[28] The Moabite deity, Chemosh, allowed Israel to conquer his people as punishment but later drove Israel out when his wrath abated. This culture, quite proximate to Israel, produced a vision of recent historical events quite similar to the Deuteronomistic notion of history.

Cultures quite contemporary with Israel were also producing literary works similar to Israel's "salvation history." It might be that Israel's historiographical style may have been the normal form of discourse among West-Semitic peoples.

C. Hittite Sources

The most significant and often underestimated historiographical materials were produced by the Hittites in the second millennium B.C. Specialists in this field have declared that Hittite historiography is equal to the later Greek historians and likewise equal or superior to the Israelite epic narratives. These scholars try to demonstrate the development of Hittite traditions toward the later Greek tradition, and set it off as a significant departure from ancient Near Eastern antecedents.[29]

Hittite sources have had many of the Greek historiographical and even modern perspectives attributed to them. Events are reported objectively and recorded for their own sake. (This is comparable to Herodotus who reported events because they were the "works of men.") Events are perceived as resulting from other events, so that a sense of development and causality manifests itself in the reports. For this reason attention to past events is necessary in order to understand the present relationship of things. Events are inter-related and inter-dependent and must be logically connected to each other. Throughout, history is the consequence of human deeds, but a higher purpose or goal may be ascertained. A sense of historical denouement can be found. In overviewing the past the reports exude a sense of objectivity, a quest for the truth, the need for evidence, and recognition that different ways to interpret past development are possible. Observation is developed to the highest degree; narratives describe particular situations in a most penetrating way. The documents may be diagrammed, as one scholar (Hubert Cancik) has done, to show their logical mode of thought and presentation. Cancik maintained that the Hittites were more logical than either Mesopotamians or Israelites, for their objectivity and approach foreshadowed the later Greeks. Hittite historiography has a sense of causality and the transitory nature of human events. Finally, in their royal reports the Hittite kings display a sense of humility and finitude not found elsewhere; their war reports show them to be human beings who must dialogue with others in the decision-making process. The Hittite annals "can justly be claimed as the oldest examples of true historiography" by one assessment.[30]

Historians are particularly impressed with the moral sensitivity displayed by these documents. Herbert Butterfield observed that not only were the reports "factual and objective," but the kings demonstrated a piety which implied a "profounder ethical sense" and the human finitude displayed "brings us to the edge of the Old Testament."[31] Burr Brundage likewise observed:

> . . . the Hittite annals are by far the most superior historiography in this case of documents. The sobriety of statement, the willingness to ascribe portions of glory to others, and the comparative lack of vain-glory all contribute to this conclusion. There is even an occasional flash of human drama.[32]

Various texts may be considered in a discussion of Hittite sources. The following are worthy of note:[33] 1) Anitta Text (1800 B.C.) is a document originally used to justify royal ascension.[34] 2) Testament of Hattushilis I (1600–1500 B.C.) is likewise a document used to legitimate royal ascension. 3) The Annals of Hattushilis I describe military actions and the conquest of cities.[35] 4) Document of Telepinus (1500 B.C.) is a text of later Hittite rulers.[36] 5) Deeds of Suppiluliuma (1350 B.C.) is a report of the deeds of one of the greatest warrior kings.[37] 6) Ten Year Annals of Mursilis II (1333–1323 B.C.) provides a basic account of the political and military events which transpired in his reign. 6) Detailed Annals of Mursilis II together with the previous document constitute what is called the Annals of Mursilis II, a full record of events in his reign.[38] And 8) Testament of Hattushilis III (1250 B.C.) is a document used to justify the irregular assumption of the throne by this individual.[39]

Most of these documents were produced by kings to justify their ascension after an interruption of royal succession. In documents like the Testament of Hattushilis I and the Annals of Mursilis II one can discover historical consciousness, rational arguments, the need to justify actions, and a concern for ascertaining the historical truth.[40] Hubert Cancik's discussion of the Annals of Mursilis II and the Deeds of Suppiluliuma is one of the most thorough attempts to demonstrate a well developed historiography.[41] Finally, the Testament of Hattushilis III introduced two new aspects into Hittite historiography: 1) history is perceived as the result of human deeds, and 2) history be directed by the gracious election of a personal deity (Ishtar).[42] In sum, Hittite documents provide the best evidence for ancient history writing in the contemporary cultural world of Israel.

This research into Hittite historiography has made an impact upon some biblical scholars. Harmut Gese and Abraham Malamat perceived that Israel's historical sense may have been derived from the Hittites. Malamat suggested that perhaps the art of history writing was introduced into Israel via a Hittite population in the city of Jerusalem, and once introduced into Israel it was "brought to artistic perfection."[43]

Certainly consideration of ancient Near Eastern historiographic literature, especially the Hittite materials, must lead to a greater appreciation of ancient Near Eastern ability. Too often biblical theologians have not paid close attention to the comparative literature.

D. Critique of Israelite Historiography

The discussion did not stop at an affirmation of ancient Near Eastern materials. Critics were quick to point out that biblical scholars too quickly praised the quality of biblical historiography, perhaps giving more credit than was deserved. Several ancient Near Eastern historians have re-evaluated the biblical material from their critical perspective.

The unevenness of Israelite historiography was readily apparent. A mixture of chronicles, sagas, legends, hero-tales, fables, and the full range of folk literary forms may be found in the Hebrew Scriptures. Israel's literature contains a mixture of "historical" and "mythical" in a way comparable to contemporary literature in the West-Semitic world and the works of Homer. All of these might be called "historical," but only in the broad sense. Israel was at the same level of development in this regard as neighboring societies.[44]

Biblical scholars often point to the Deuteronomistic History as the classic example of historiography in the Hebrew Bible, for it covers a long period of time with a critical theological criteria for evaluating the events, kings, and political motivations of the people. Yet ancient historians can point to the same type of literature in the ancient Near East. Worthy of close comparison with the Deuteronomistic History are documents such as the Babylonian Chronicle, Weidner Chronicle, and the later Egyptian Demotic Chronicle (which censures pharaohs of the Twenty-Eighth through the Thirtieth Dynasties). All these texts survey a significant amount of history and condemn rulers for their failure to measure up to certain religious or moral standards.[45]

Hubert Cancik, who has offered a most thorough observation of Hittite materials, goes so far as to affirm the superiority of Hittite historiography over that of Israel. Hittite sources have a sense of objectivity, a quest for the truth, logical progression, causality, all of which are lacking in the Israelite sources according to his assessment. Among Hittites and the later Greeks there appear words to denote objective truth, but for the Hebrew Bible the notion appears with the subjective meaning of faithfulness. Israelite materials were produced and redacted by theologians who lacked an objective distance from the events they recalled, rather they reviewed the past to find a basis for understanding human sin and divine forgiveness. Authors of the biblical texts were anonymous in contrast to their Hittite and Greek counterparts as a result of their deep religious piety. The Hittite and Greek materials display a strong sense of individual consciousness because of the importance they place not only upon the individual but also upon the human perspective in general. The absence of such individual consciousness among Israelite authors is directly related to a loss of objectivity. A sense of causality is not found within individual biblical narratives, but rather was inserted as an editorial framework by the Deuteronomistic Historians. By way of contrast this sense of causality may be observed directly within the accounts found in the Hittite annals. This is due, in part, to the poverty of the Hebrew language, which lacks syntactical connectives (causal, result, purpose, and negative causal) and has only the simple connective *waw*, "and." Since purpose and result cannot be easily expressed in Hebrew, real historiography could not have developed in that culture.[46]

Cancik analyzed several Old Testament texts and concluded that Hebrew narratives have the content and structure of historical annals, but they lack the proper linguistic tools to make discerning and nuanced observations about past events. The Hebrew Scriptures offer no parallels to Hittite or Greek sources until the Hellenistic period when Greek influence shaped the modes of Jewish discourse. II Maccabees is Israel's first true historiographical work with an objective, factual, and fully evaluative approach. Herein is found an objective quest for truth. Had not all the older materials been so theologized, perhaps the earlier annals and reports of the Israelite monarchs might have evolved into a true historiography.[47]

Thus Cancik evaluated Hittite, Israelite, and Greek materials in relation to each other and found that all have a sense of historical criticism mixed with the old mythic tradition. In his evaluation he observed that the spectrum of development moved from Mesopotamian royal reports to later Hittite historical reports. Israel was more advanced than the Mesopotamian sources, but clearly inferior to the Hittites. The Greeks were the culmination of the evolution of historiography in the ancient world, they inherited this developing process from the ancient Near East most probably through the mediation of the Hittites and their successor states.[48]

John Van Seters also engaged in a thorough study of ancient Near Eastern historiography. As noted earlier he maintained that historiography arose from annals, royal reports, military lists, monumental inscriptions, and other documents produced by the royal courts. By way of contrast biblical theologians sought the origin of historiography in epic literature. This bias led them to elevate the biblical narratives and denigrate ancient annals as a form of history writing. Van Seters responded by pointing out the similarity of ancient Near Eastern and biblical materials in terms of their historiographic quality.[49] In particular, he affirmed that true historiography did not arise in Israel until the era of the exile, making it contemporary with the rise of Greek historiography. The Deuteronomistic History was Israel's first authentic historical document. This literature was produced by creative and brilliant historians, and Van Seters would credit more originality to this person or school than even was attributed by Martin Noth.[50] What Van Seters affirmed in response to the biblical theologians was that historiography arose not in the time of the United Monarchy under David or Solomon with the epic traditions, rather it was a late and exilic phenomenon.[51] If so, a contrast with the ancient Near East is vitiated simply by the lateness of the total process.

Though his general conclusions were similar, the assessment of J. J. M. Roberts differed from Van Seters on the question of the Deuteronomistic Historian. He felt this biblical tradition merely placed blocks of pre-existing literature together. But in this regard Israelite authors and editors were comparable to ancient Near Eastern historians who functioned similarly in the creation of their annals. Roberts pointed out that if we criticize ancient historians for merely placing blocks of older sources together, we must admit that the style of the Deuteronomistic Historian is really no different, so that history writing in the ancient Near East and Israel are truly comparable.[52]

E. Conclusion

Ancient Near Eastern historians strongly suggested that a well developed historiographic tradition existed in the second millennium B.C. which was carried down into the first millennium B.C. sources. In this light Israel's historical perspective could hardly be seen as unique. One might especially cite significant historiographic works produced by Israel's most proximate neighbors, such as in Moab. Biblical scholars simply failed to take this comparative literature into account when speculating upon Israel's notion of salvation history.

The approach of biblical scholars has been criticized for its myopic approach. The unfair glorification of biblical sources combined with criticism or indifference to ancient Near Eastern sources has aroused the ire of ancient Near Eastern scholars. Nicolas Wyatt aptly concluded:

> Such judgments seem not only to fly in the face of such fairly obvious historiographical and annalistic evidence as survives, but also to prejudge whole cultures on the basis of conceptions of the biblical view which are themselves questionable.[53]

A critical observer from the area of classical studies summarized the entire debate with the following insightful comments:

> There is something of a consensus among historians of historiography that the peoples of the ancient Near East, with the usual exception of Israel, had an "ahistorical" mentality. Such a generalization needs considerable refinement before it can be accepted. . . . In Mesopotamia there are obviously various literary genres (the most important being the chronicle series) which stood in some relation to what is commonly called historiography.[54]

It is this refinement of our old theories which needs to be undertaken, and which this work will seek discuss.

Notes

1. Westermann, "Grenze," *op. cit.*, pp. 489–496; Cancik, *Wahrheit, op. cit.*, pp. 72–76, and *Grundzüge der hethitischen und alttes-*

47

tamentlichten Geschichtsschreibung (Wiesbaden: Harrassowitz, 1976), pp. 8–10.

2. Frank Moore Cross, *Canaanite Myth and Hebrew Epic: Essays in the History of the Religion of Israel* (Cambridge, Massachusetts: Harvard University, 1973), p. ix.

3. Cancik, *Grundzüge, op. cit.*, p. 59; Butterfield, *History, op. cit.*, pp. 44–79; and Van Seters, *History, op. cit.*, pp. 55–208.

4. Brundage, "Birth of Clio," *op. cit.*, p. 200; Joachim Krecher and Hans Peter Müller, "Vergangenheitsinteresse in Mesopotamien und Israel," *Saeculum* 26 (1975): 24; and Cancik, *Grundzüge, op. cit.*, p. 47.

5. Harmut Gese, "The Idea of History in the Ancient Near East and the Old Testament," *The Bultmann School of Biblical Interpretation: New Directions?*, ed. Robert Funk, Journal for Theology and the Church, vol. 1 (New York: Harper and Row, 1965), p. 49; Cancik, *Wahrheit, op. cit.*, p. 51; and J. Roy Porter, "Old Testament Historiography," *Tradition and Interpretation: Essays by Members of the Society for Old Testament Study,* ed. George Anderson (Oxford, England: Clarendon, 1979), p. 128;

6. Cancik, *Wahrheit, op. cit.*, p. 47; Krecher and Müller, "Vergangenheitsinteresse," *op. cit.*, p. 24; Porter, "Historiography," *op. cit.*, p. 128; and William Hallo, "Sumerian Historiography," *History, Historiography and Interpretation: Studies in biblical and cuneiform literatures,* eds. Hayim Tadmor and Moshe Weinfeld (Jerusalem: Magnes, 1984), pp. 9–20.

7. Hayim Tadmor, "Observations on Assyrian Historiography," *Essays on the Ancient Near East in Memory of Jacob Joel Finkelstein,* ed. Maria de Jong Ellis, Memoirs of the Connecticut Academy of Arts and Sciences, vol. 19 (Hamden, Connecticut: Archon, 1977), pp. 209–213.

8. Jacob Joel Finkelstein, "Mesopotamian Historiography," *Proceedings of the American Philosophical Society* 107 (1963): 461–472.

9. Speiser, "Idea of History," *op. cit.*, pp. 55–57, pointed to the examples of accounts by Yasmah-Addu of Mari and Tulkulti-Ninurta I of Assyria.

10. Roberts, "Myth Versus History," *op. cit.*, pp. 3–4.

11. *Ibid.*, p. 4, at which point he criticized the observations of Lambert, "Destiny and divine intervention in Babylon and Israel," *Old Testament Studies* 17 (1972): 70–71.

12. Krecher and Müller, "Vergangenheitsinteresse," pp. 23–24.

13. Samuel Noah Kramer, *From the Tablets at Sumer* (Indian Hills, Colorado: Falcon's Wing Press, 1956), p. 267; and Albrektson, *History, op. cit.*, p. 24.

14. Kramer, *The Sumerians: Their History, Culture, and Character* (Chicago: University of Chicago, 1963), p. 62. Krecher and Müller, "Vergangenheitsinteresse," *op. cit.*, pp. 20–21, would wish to include the Naru literature of Sargon and Naram-Sin for consideration because of the historical consciousness they believe is found therein.

15. Brundage, "Birth of Clio," *op. cit.*, p. 209.

16. Robert Biggs, "More Babylonian Prophecies," *Iraq* 29 (1967): 117–119; and Herbert Hunger and S. A. Kaufman, "A New Akkadian Prophecy Text," *Journal of the American Oriental Society* 95 (1975): 371–375.

17. Eva Osswald, "Altorientalische Parallelen zur deuteronomistischen Geschichtsbetrachtung," *Mitteilungen des Institutes für Orientforschung* 15 (1969): 288–293; Krecher and Müller, "Vergangenheitsinteresse," *op. cit.*, p. 25; Butterfield, *History, op. cit.*, p. 40; and Van Seters, *History, op. cit.*, p. 88.

18. Gese, "Idea," *op. cit.*, pp. 56–58.

19. Brundage, "Birth of Clio," *op. cit.*, p. 208.

20. Roberts, "Nebuchadnezzar I's Elamite Crisis in Theological Perspective," *Essays on the Ancient Near East, op. cit.*, pp. 183–187; and Van Seters, *History, op. cit.*, pp. 95, 97.

21. Michael Rowton, "Chronology. II. Ancient Western Asia," *The Cambridge Ancient History*, vol. 1, pt. 1: *Prolegomena and Prehistory*, 3rd ed., eds. I. E. S. Edwards, C. J. Gadd, and N. G. L. Hammond (Cambridge, England: Cambridge University, 1970), p. 196; and A. Kirk Grayson, "Assyria: Ashur-dan II to Ashur-Nirari V (934–745 B.C.)," *The Cambridge Ancient History*, vol. 3, pt. 1: *The Prehistory of the Balkans; and the Middle East and the Aegean world, tenth to the eighth centuries B.C.*, 3rd ed., eds. John Boardman, I. E. S. Edwards, N. G. L. Hammond, and E. Sollberger (Cambridge, England: Cambridge University, 1982), pp. 242, 277–278.

22. Brundage, "Birth of Clio," *op. cit.*, pp. 208–209, called it a "welter of disparate facts," so factual in its account did it appear to him; and Van Seters, *History, op. cit.*, pp. 80–92, 294–297.

23. Grayson, "Assyria," *op. cit.*, p. 242.

24. Albrecht Goetze, "The Hittites and Syria," *The Cambridge Ancient History*, vol. 2, pt. 2: *History of the Middle East and the*

Aegean Region c. 1380–1000, eds. I. E. S. Edwards, N. G. L. Hammond, C. J. Gadd, and E. Sollberger (Cambridge, England: Cambridge University, 1975), P. 272.

25. Saggs, *The Might that was Assyria* (London: Sidgwick and Jackson, 1984), pp. 265–266.

26. Nicholas Wyatt, "Some Observations on the Idea of History Among the West Semitic Peoples," *Ugarit Forschungen* 11 (1979): 828.

27. *Ibid.,* pp. 825–832.

28. Albrektson, *History, op. cit.,* p. 7.

29. Cancik, *Wahrheit, op. cit.,* pp. 17–130, and *Grundzüge, op. cit.,* pp. 3–213; and Hans Güterbock, "Hittite Historiography: A Survey," *History, Historiography and Interpretation, op. cit.,* pp. 21–35.

30. Gese, "Idea," *op. cit.,* p. 59; Cancik, *Wahrheit, op. cit.,* pp. 58–59, 71–78, and *Grundzüge, op. cit.,* pp. 8, 46, 130; and Goetze, "Hittites," *op. cit.,* pp. 271–272, who made the quoted assertion.

31. Butterfield, *History, op. cit.,* pp. 68–69.

32. Brundage, "Birth of Clio," *op. cit.,* p. 213.

33. Cancik, *Wahrheit, op. cit.,* pp. 46–65, and *Grundzüge, op. cit.,* pp. 101–167, provided the best evaluation of this literature; Harry Hoffner, "Propaganda and Political Justification in Hittite Historiography," *Unity and Diversity, op. cit.,* pp. 49–62; and Van Seters, *History, op. cit.,* pp. 105–126.

34. Güterbock, "Die historische Tradition und ihre literarische Gestaltung bei Babyloniern und Hethitern bis 1200," *Zeitschrift für Assyriologie* 42 (1938): 134–145.

35. *Idem.,* "Sargon of Akkad Mentioned by Hattushili I of Hatti," *Journal of Cuneiform Studies* 18 (1964): 1–6; Hoffner, "Histories and Historians of the Ancient Near East: The Hittites," *Orientalia* 49 (1980): 293–299; and Van Seters, *History, op. cit.,* pp. 107, 114.

36. Hoffner, "Histories," *op. cit.,* pp. 306–308; and Van Seters, *History, op. cit.,* pp. 115–116.

37. Güterbock, "The Deeds of Suppiluliuma as told by his Son, Mursili II," *Journal of Cuneiform Studies* 10 (1956): 41–50, 59–68, 75–85, 90–98, 107–130, provided an excellent evaluation of this text.

38. *Ibid.,* and "Tradition," *op. cit.,* pp. 95–96; Hoffner, "Histories," *op. cit.,* pp. 311–315; and Van Seters, *History, op. cit.,* pp. 109–111.

39. Hoffner, "Histories," *op. cit.,* pp. 315–316; and Herbert Mar-

lin Wolf, "The Apology of Hattushilis Compared with Other Politicial Self-Justifications of the Ancient Near East" (Ann Arbor, Michigan: University Microfilms, 1967), p. 223.

40. Cancik, *Wahrheit, op. cit.*, pp. 82–84; and Tadmor, "Autobiographical Apology in the Royal Assyrian Literature," *History, Historiography and Interpretation, op. cit.*, pp. 36–57.

41. Cancik, *Grundzüge, op. cit.*, pp. 101–167.

42. Idem, *Wahrheit, op. cit.*, p. 76.

43. Abraham Malamat, "Doctrine of Causality in Hittite and biblical Historiography: a parallel," *Vetus Testamentum* 5 (1955): 1; and Gese, "Idea," *op. city.*, pp. 65–102.

44. Krecher and Müller, "Vergangenheitsinteresse," *op. cit.*, pp. 30–44, found little difference in their overview of cross-cultural materials; and Wyatt, "Observations," *op. cit.*, p. 831.

45. Osswald, "Parallelen," *op. cit.*, pp. 287, 293–295.

46. Cancik, *Wahrheit, op. cit.*, pp. 90–108, and *Grundzüge, op. cit.*, pp. 28, 41, 46, 185–190.

47. Cancik, *Wahrheit, op. cit.*, pp. 7–130, and *Grundzüge, op. cit.*, pp. 185–213.

48. Cancik, *Grundzüge, op. cit.*, pp. 34 et passim.

49. Van Seters, *History, op. cit.*, pp. 1–362.

50. *Ibid.*, p. 359, in contrast to Noth, *The Deuteronomistic History*, Journal for the Study of the Old Testament Supplement Series, vol. 15 (Sheffield, England: JSOT Press, 1981), pp. 1–99.

51. Van Seters, *History, op. cit.*, pp. 354–362, and he also analyzed material in Samuel and Kings to reach the conclusion that the Deuteronomistic Historian was Israel's first true historian.

52. Roberts, "Myth Versus History," *op. cit.*, p. 4. Cf. Ziony Zevit, "Deuteronomistic Historiography in I Kings 12–2 Kings 17 and the Reinvestiture of the Israelian Cult," *Journal for the Study of the Old Testament* 32 (1985): 57–59, who noted the similarity of cultic agenda in biblical and Mesopotamian histories.

53. Wyatt, "Observations," *op. cit.*, p. 825.

54. Robert Drews, "Sargon, Cyrus and Mesopotamian Folk History," *Journal of Near Eastern Studies* 33 (1974): 387.

Chapter 5
Salvation History Themes in the Ancient Near East

Not only did ancient Near Eastern scholars seek to affirm the presence of authentic historical perspectives and the existence of historiographic literature, they also sought to indicate the presence of ancient Near Eastern parallels with specific themes isolated by biblical theologians as theologomena unique to Israel. Though a consensus arose among critics concerning the presence of historiographical literature in the ancient world, not all concurred that there is commonality between Israel and the ancient Near East in regard to particular themes germane to the salvation history model. But most would agree that the commonality of many themes indicated that the same general worldview tended to predominate in Israel as was found in the rest of the ancient world. On this discussion the fullest presentation has been offered by Bertil Albrektson (*History and the Gods,* 1967) and H. W. F. Saggs (*The Encounter with the Divine in Mesopotamia and Israel*, 1978). The following discussion represents a selection of the key observations made by these and other scholars.

A. Ancient Near Eastern Deities Acted In Human Affairs

In the ancient Near East the gods could be seen as intervening in human affairs in a way which we would call "acting in history." Very early onward Mesopotamians believed that cultic and political offenses might cause the gods to punish kings, dynasties, cities, and countries in the historical or political realm of affairs. Many of the same images were used in Egypt, Mesopotamia, the land of the Hittites, and Israel to describe this divine intervention, especially in metaphors of warfare. Furthermore, the idea of a personal deity who relates personally to the king, city, or people in order to defeat enemies was articulated quite commonly also. (A good example of the latter is how Ishtar guided Hattushilis III over his enemies to become king—Testament of Hattushilis III).

By the first millennium B. C. "the gods, seen as kings and rulers, were no longer powers in nature only, they became powers in human affairs—in history."[2] Mesopotamian texts especially show the gods to be more than elemental natural forces, they governed all domains of life, history, and nature. Particular deities of whom this may be said include Enlil, Marduk, Ashur, and Ninurta.[3] By our standards the ancient Near Eastern perception viewed the gods as acting in history. Our distinction between divine activity in history and nature is an artificial construct, for in both Israel and the ancient Near East divine activity was experienced in both dimensions with no clear distinction.[4] As Bertil Albrektson succinctly stated:

> . . . both conceptions (history and nature) are very ancient in the Semitic religions, and that Israel has here a share in a common heritage; . . . the very distinction between nature and history seems little relevant and is not likely to have been recognized at all.[5]

The ability of the gods to intervene in human affairs is best demonstrated by reports of divine activity in military and political events, especially victory or defeat on the battlefield. A number of texts can be offered for consideration:

1) A Sumerian text from around 2400 B.C. describes the tensions between the city-states of Umma and Lagash and the activity of the gods. A selection of that text reads as follows:

> The Ummaite who (at any time) will cross the boundary ditch of Ningirsu (and) the boundary ditch of Nanshe in order to take to himself fields and farms by force . . . may Enlil destroy him;

54

may Ningirsu, after hurling his great Shush-net on him, bring down on him his lofty hand (and) his lofty foot.[6]

2) The Sumerian Lamentation over the Destruction of Ur is the longest example of a lament over the fall of a city or a political dynasty. A few representative lines reflect the tenor of the entire composition:

Verily Anu changed not this work;
Verily Enlil with its "It is good; so be it" soothed not my heart.
The utter destruction of my city verily they directed,
The utter destruction of Ur verily they directed;
That its people be killed, as its fate verily they decreed.
. . .
Anu changes not his command;
Enlil alters not the command which he had issued.[7]

3) The Legend of Naram-Sin from the early second millennium B.C. is a form of *narû* literature, and it raises a lament for the demise of the great Akkadian king Naram-Sin resulting from his act of sacrilege. A further variation on this text is found in the form of the Cuthean Legend. In the Cuthean Legend the king laments the action of the deity when he says, "I despaired, I groaned, I grieved, I grew faint. Thus I thought: 'What has God brought upon my reign.' "[8]

4) The Curse on Akkad is an example of how the gods chose to punish the nation in the course of history, and it is often discussed as an example of Mesopotamian historiography. Selected lines form the text reflect the actions of the gods:

Holy Inanna forsook the shrine Agade,
Like a warrior hastening to (his) weapon,
She went forth against the city in battle (and) combat,
She attacked as if it were a foe
. . .
Enlil brought down from the mountain.
In vast numbers, like locusts, they covered the earth.[9]

5) The Hittite account, Ritual Before Battle, contains a plea for the Hittite gods to wipe out the enemy Kashkeans, and it

demonstrates the belief that impending actions are determined by divine powers. The plea reads as follows:

> Blot out the Kashkean country, O gods! Let every single god take thought for his place of worship and win it back! Let Zithariyas win back his place of worship! Let him again roam those countries.[10]

6) The Hittite Proclamation of Telepinus perceives the victory by the king over his enemies to be a gift of the gods. The expression found therein, "the gods delivered it into my hands," resonates comparably with similar biblical expressions.[11]

7) In the Amarna letters Tushratta, king of the Mitanni in Syria, uses the expression, "Teshub, my lord gave them into my hand and I beat them" (Amarna tablet #17, line 32). Again we are reminded of similar language in the Deuteronomistic History.[12]

8) Mursilis II (1339–1306 B.C.), a Hittite king, attributes to the goddess his ability to conquer foreign countries according to the report in the Ten Year Annals. He states:

> And the Sun-goddess of Arinna heard my prayer and came to my aid, and in ten years from the time when I sat on my father's throne I conquered these hostile countries and destroyed them.[13]

Mursilis II also said the Hattian storm god brought the people of Kurustama to the country of Egypt in the famous Plague Prayer.[14] The imagery clearly reminds us of Exodus references in the biblical tradition.

9) Tukulti-Ninurta I (1244–1208 B.C.) speaks of divine intervention in the temple inscriptions to the god Ashur at Kar-Tukulti-Ninurta, a significant site for new building construction by this king. He invokes a curse in the inscription to protect the site:

> . . . may Assur ruin his kingdom, shatter his weapons, and bring about the defeat of his armies; may he diminish his boundaries, and decree the cutting short of his reign; may he make his days sad and his years evil; his name and his seed may he destroy from the land.[15]

10) In the later Assyrian work, the Tukulti-Ninurta Epic, the Babylonian gods are said to have deserted Babylon for Assyria. The motif of divine abandonment is quite common in many laments, both in reference to individuals and cities. Some selected lines from the Tukulti-Ninurta Epic read as follows:

> Of the lord of all the lands, his Enlilship was distressed with Nippur.
> To the habitation of Dur-Kurigalzu he does not approach.
> Marduk abandoned his august sanctuary, (the city),
> He cursed the city of his love.[16]

11) A prayer uttered by Tiglath-Pileser I (1115-1077 B.C.) of Assyria speaks of divine action in history and nature. The king prayed the following:

> . . . may Anu and Adad truly turn unto me . . . In battle and combat may they lead me in safety. All the lands of my enemies, the lands of rulers and princes who hate me may they bring into submission under my feet.[17]

12) Nabu-apla-iddina of Babylon in the ninth century B.C. uses similar language in a warning inscription at a re-endowed sun temple at Sippar. He calls forth a mighty curse from the sun god, Shamash, and other deities:

> . . . as for that man by the command of Shamash, Aya and Bunene, lords of the decision, the great gods, may his name perish, may his seed be destroyed, through starvation and hunger may his life come to an end, may his corpse be cast aside, and may he have no burial.[18]

13) A state latter of the official, Kuduru, during the reign of Ashurbanipal (669–627 B.C.) of Assyria describes the actions of the deity Ashur as being effective in human affairs. Concerning an individual named Upaqu the official states:

> Bel, Nabu, Ishtar of Erech and Nana may from sunrise to the sunset utterly destroy him and deliver (him) into the hands of the king my Lord (letter 26, lines 6–8).[19]

57

14) The Erra Epic, a major Akkadian work in the seventh century B.C., interprets the fall of Babylon as a historical disaster produced by divine agents because of the neglect of Erra's worship. The author envisions a future restoration of the city, which might remind us of the oracles of Deutero-Isaiah (Isaiah 40–55):

> Let the sparse people of the land multiply again,
> Let short and tall alike tread its road,
> Let crippled Akkad throw down the mighty Sutû.[20]

Other texts worthy of brief mention due to similar allusions might include inscriptions by Tuthmosis III (ANET 374), Hammurabi (ANET 165, 270), and Esarhaddon (ANET 450).[21]

The notion of the gods acting to control human events occurs in diverse forms of literature ranging from many different eras. Types include historical texts, hymns, prayers, laments, and rituals. The verbal forms in many of these texts are causative, the same mood used in Hebrew to describe the actions of Yahweh.[22]

A special type of text may also be noted: several accounts imply that the deities work particularly through the agency of the king. Kings are representatives of the gods to do their work in the world, so that all the activities of the king testify indirectly to the historical direction of the various deities. Some brief examples might be listed:[23] 1) Utuhegal, king of Uruk in the third millennium B.C., defeated the Gutians at the command of Enlil. 2) Utu, the sun god, selected Nur-Adad (1865–1850 B.C.) to restore the city of Larsa in Mesopotamia. 3) Nebuchadrezzar I (1124–1103 B.C.) is sent by the gods to avenge the defeat of Akkad, the poetic title for Babylon in the Kassite period. 4) Nabu-apla-iddina of Babylon (ninth century B.C.) is likewise sent forth to avenge Akkad, or Babylon. 5) Shalmaneser of Assyria (858–824 B.C.) extols his heroic accomplishment as though the gods performed them through his agency (ANET 277). 6) Tiglath-Pileser I (1115–1077 B.C.) declares that the deity gave the throne to him and his family forever, a promise which reminds us of the Davidic Covenant in the Israelite traditions. 7) Esarhaddon (680–669 B.C.) also speaks of the eternal commitment of the gods to his dynasty, and the kings were the agents of the gods in this world (ANET 289, 449–450). 8) A dynastic promise to a king in the Aramaic inscription of Zakir has the deity proclaim to the ruler, ". . . it was I who made you king . . . I shall deliver you from all (those kings who) have forced a siege upon you."[24]

On the basis of these and other examples Bertil Albrektson concluded:

> . . . historical events are . . . caused by supernatural agents, the gods create history. The idea that their main sphere of activity is nature does not even begin to emerge; here they are all concerned with what happens in the relations of states and men.[25]

B. Ancient Near Eastern Divine Plans for Human History

Not only did ancient Near Eastern deities intervene in specific events of human history, they had plans for the general direction of history, so that specific occasions of divine activity were not random but rather part of a greater unfolding scenario. This notion is an extension of those observations concerning divine actions in human affairs, and not all historians would agree to it. But several scholars, especially those familiar with Assyrian texts, defend it. This thesis is certainly a direct challenge to the cyclic and linear stereotypes offered by biblical scholars. Some biblical theologians admitted that ancient Near Eastern deities intervened in historical events occasionally, but they denied the existence of an overall plan or ultimate goal in human history. Ancient Near Eastern scholars perceived that some texts do indeed imply long range goals for human history were present. If so, cyclic patterns could not be said to typify the ancient Near Eastern notion of history.[26]

The debate becomes one of subjective interpretation of the texts. Some critics would still maintain that the ancient gods did not pursue purposeful action for a sustained period of time. However, if one were able to discount Babylonian chronicles and Assyrian ideas about the rule of Ashur, perhaps not even the Israelite materials would be able to qualify as "history" under the same strict criteria. Both the ancient Near Easterners and the Israelites envisioned their deities as executing purposeful influence in the arena of human affairs for a sustained period of time for specific reasons and goals. Such activity should certainly be called a divine plan in the general sense.

The best cultures for observation are probably the Hittite and Assyrian. In the Hittite Apology of Hattushilis III one can sense that Ishtar has a divine plan for Hattushilis III and she sustains her activity over a period of years on his behalf.[27] Assyrian texts in the first millennium B.C. offer the best evidence for a divine plan, however. Assyrians believed themselves to be heirs to a divine plan which would exalt them as a universal dominion which would absorb all the neighboring peoples; hence, their policy of human deportation was really a systematic attempt to merge various populations into one people eventually. Assyrian imperialism was built "on a particular theology of Ashur, the view that the god had a plan for his land and that he was separate from his land and his people."[28] One senses an echo of the classical prophets of Israel with their vision of Yahweh's universal rule. If the above mentioned opinion of H. W. F. Saggs is correct, one might hypothesize the origin of Israelite notions to be found in these contemporary Assyrian values.

A piece of Assyrian literature worthy of consideration in this regard is the Tukulti-Ninurta Epic, a document from the later Assyrian Empire. This politically inspired literature justified the Assyrian conquest of Babylon in the seventh century B.C. while accepting the influence of Babylonian acculturation. In its present form, as theological-political literature, it is comparable to literature of the United Monarchy in Israel which justifies political ascendancy in Palestine while accepting rapprochement with Canaanite culture.[29]

60

In addition there are a number of other examples which may be cited to illustrate the image of deities who have some plan for human affairs:[30]

1) In the Curse of Akkad the god Enlil brings the Gutians to ravage the city of Akkad for the sacrilege committed by Naram-Sin to the shrine in Nippur.

2) The Weidner Chronicle demonstrates belief in the continued activities of gods over many years bringing punishment upon various Mesopotamian kings and dynasties.

3) The Apology of Hattushilis III (1275–1250 B.C.) justifies his ascension to the throne over a period of time through complex and sometimes cruel political machinations, all of which were condoned by the goddess Ishtar in dream theophanies to the king.

4) The Annals of Mursilis II are similar to those of Hattushilis III. Together both of these documents remind readers of the Succession Narrative in II Samuel 9–20 and I Kings 1–2 in that the gods act through the everyday affairs and court politics.

5) In the Erra Epic the restoration and triumph of Babylon is described over a period of time worthy to be characterized as a "divine plan in human history."

6) Esarhaddon of Assyria (680–669 B.C.) describes how Enlil became angry and punished Babylon, sent them into a seventy year "exile" with the destruction of the city at the hands of the Assyrians, but the deity restored them when Esarhaddon rebuilt the city (text Babylon A–G).

In addition to these examples there is the custom of fixing the fates for the coming year in the Babylonian New Year's festival or the *akitu* festival. Herein the will of the gods was determined for significant events in the upcoming year. The ritual texts refer to the use of "Tablets of Destiny," which are involved in this process of fixing the fates of the people for the year. The existence and use of these "Tablets of Destiny," whatever they may have been, in a general way implies the perception of a divine plan for the course of human affairs, which could be discerned by divination. Albrektson noted that since one could find nothing in the Hebrew Bible comparable to these traditions or the use of such tablets:

> One is almost tempted to say that in certain respects we are more justified in speaking of a fixed divine plan in history in Mesopotamian religion than in the Old Testament.[31]

Other scholars, inluding H. W. F. Saggs, especially emphasized the Assyrian texts where kings claim divine legitimation for their ensuing dynasties. For Saggs it was apparent that:

> . . . the gods of Assyria had a plan in history effected through the continuance of one particular dynasty.[32]

The general conclusion would be that Israel and the neighboring cultures all "know the idea of purposeful divine actions toward a definite goal in history."[33]

In conjunction with this same line of argument some scholars tried to minimize the significance of the notion of a divine plan in the Hebrew Scriptures, thus affirming that Israel was in greater continuity with neighboring cultures in this understanding. Albrektson believed that the biblical text affirms a divine purpose but not a divine plan; the notion of a plan must be used only in a weakened sense to describe material in the Yahwist, Priestly Editors, the Chronicler, and the Prophets. Wherever words which might mean "plan" are used in the biblical text, they are really quite vague and cannot undergird the notion of a fixed divine plan from beginning to end. There may be different divine plans, but not one, in the various biblical traditions. Only in apocalyptic literature does there appear a truly uniform divine plan for all history.[34] Thus we find "the view that Yahweh acts purposefully in what happens" or in a "limited series of events, an episode or an epoch;" but we cannot find "History with a capital H" or the "idea that history as a whole is heading for a definite goal along a road laid out according to a fixed plan" or "all history, the entire succession of events from creation to consummation" or "universal history."[35]

C. Divine Word of Ancient Near Eastern Deities Active in History

The ancient Near East also appears to have had a concept of the "divine word which was efficacious in both nature (creation and conservation) and history."[36] This control over all realms of human existence was perceived by the peoples of the ancient Near East as a "mighty and terrifying power . . . effective in all spheres of life."[37] Mesopotamians believed that if the word of the king had power, the word of the deity was even greater. The word of the deity reflected the rank and prestige of that deity by being an appropriately powerful unit of energy.[38] Likewise for the Hittites the word of the deity represented divine will, and their similarity to the Israelite prophets is even greater in this regard.[39]

The most celebrated accounts are those Egyptian texts of the Memphite theological tradition with their abstract notion of the Word. Though the texts which we possess come from as late as 700 B.C., the material presumably reflects beliefs of the earlier periods. Herein the deity Ptah conceives the other gods through the thought of his heart and the utterance of his mouth. (The image reminds us of Genesis 1.) The Word of Ptah was an order or direction for cosmic or human affairs according to the Memphite theology. In later developments the "Word of Ptah" was associated with written literature, or rather the will of the gods became expressed in written texts.[40] (We are reminded again of Israel and how the "Word of the Lord" evolved from association with oral proclamations to written literature.)

In Mesopotamia a similarly significant creation account features the powerful and creative word of the deity. In the Enuma Elish, the Babylonian account of creation, Marduk is made king, and by his word a garment is made to vanish and then reappear.[41] Though critics have disputed the comparison with the creative word spoken by God in Genesis 1 to create the world, because Marduk's actions seem more like magic than real creation, nonetheless the comparison does indicate that the spoken word of deities in other cultures had power.

Albrektson offered a number of examples taken from different genres of literature and thereby concluded that the divine word was consistently used throughout the ancient Near East as a "means of controlling events and so of governing the course of history."[42] This is quite similar to the Israelite view of the divine word which proclaims Yahweh's will and interprets history.[43] In the light of this general discussion a biblical theologian, Frederick Moriarity, concluded:

> The Old Testament inherited, with only slight modifications, this dynamic notion of the efficacious word applying it according to its own theological needs and within the limits of its orthodoxy.[44]

Furthermore, we recall the critique of James Barr and other critics of the Biblical Theology Movement who noted that the biblical text is really a revelatory word which interprets history rather than being an account of history, and this implies that "word revelation" is an even more significant theologomena for Israel. If so, an even greater degree of similarity is to be noted between Israel and the contemporary ancient Near Eastern cultures.

D. History as Revelation in the Ancient Near East

A further extension of the ideas presented in the first three sections of this chapter is the conclusion that historical events may be perceived as an actual direct form of divine revelation in the ancient Near Eastern texts. In other words, history is revelation. This is a rather bold thesis, and it appears to be defended exclusively by Bertil Albrektson. If he is correct, he has gone beyond the position that many biblical theologians would hold in regard to the nature of the biblical documents. To declare that history is itself revelation of a deity is to use the language that one anticipates from Wolfhart Pannenberg and Jürgen Moltmann. Nevertheless, Albrektson defends his position with a number of examples. The classic instance would be a text wherein the anger of the deity is demonstrated toward a city, king, or dynasty for some cultic offense, and punishment transpires in the form of a political disaster. The disaster or punishment would be the actual revelation or self-manifestation of that deity.

Albrektson cited the following examples:[45]

1) In the Curse of Akkad the barbarian Gutians punish the Akkadians for the sin of Naram-Sin, and this represents the judgment of Enlil in history for cultic offenses.

2) In the Babylonian Weidner Chronicle various kings like Sargon and Naram-Sin commit an offense and thereby lose Marduk's favor. His anger manifests itself in historical disasters as a theophany. (We are reminded of the Deuteronomistic History passing judgment on various kings for their failure to acknowledge correct worship in the Temple in Jerusalem.)

3) In the Proclamation of Telepinus the Hittite text affirms that the gods punish all people, even kings, for their sins, through various historical disasters.

4) In the Plague Prayer of Mursilis II (1339–1306 B.C.) the Hittite king perceives that plagues and foreign invasions are punishments in history for some unknown sin. The parallel with the plague brought upon Israel by Saul's sin in I Samuel 21 has been mentioned commonly in the discussion of this text. Albrektson made the following observation:

> The idea of national misfortune as divine punishment for a collective guilt which transcends the individual generations is an important element of the Deuteronomic view of history, but obviously it is not a distinctive feature.[46]

5) Tukulti-Ninurta I (1244–1208 B.C.) of Assyria defeated Kashtiliash IV (1242–1235 B.C.) of Kassite Babylon and declared this to be the judgment of the Babylonian deities who were angry with their king, Kashtiliash IV, for breaking oaths which he had made.

6) The Mesha Stone of Moab interprets Israel's defeat of Moab to be a result of Chemosh's anger. The anger was

manifest in defeat, but when the deity became gracious again, Israel was driven out by Moab.

7) In the Erra Epic of Assyria the downfall of Babylon is interpreted as a manifestation of Ishtar's wrath and divine judgment.

8) Esarhaddon (680–669 B.C.) of Assyria describes the later restoration of the fallen city of Babylon as the sign of divine mercy of the god Enlil or Marduk.

9) Ashurbanipal (668–627 B.C.) of Assyria views Assyrian military victories in his annals as divine judgment upon the enemies. In particular, the defeat of Arab tribes occurred because the Arabs had broken their oaths, and the wrath of the gods was manifest upon them.

After discussing these examples Albrektson can conclude:

> The doctrine of moral retribution is a "stock interpretation" of defeat and disaster in the ancient Near East.[47]

Such retribution is perceived to be clear example of historical events as divine revelation. The implication for the biblical materials would be clear. The grand Deuteronomistic History which interprets the successive political difficulties of the Israelite nation states as a result of sin, and especially the negligence of the pure worship of Yahweh in the Temple of Jerusalem, would be nothing more than a typical ancient Near Eastern apologetic text.

The particular thesis which Albrektson defends by listing and discussing these texts is that history is revelation in the ancient texts, especially the manifestation of anger by a particular deity. His evaluation is highly subjective, however, and few would agree with him. The texts listed above might simply be perceived as demonstrating that the gods act through historical disasters. To say that the actual disaster which befalls king, dynasty, city, or people is an actual manifestation of the deity or the essential nature of the deity might be pushing the texts beyond what they are really saying. Thus this final category may be the weakest argument presented by critics of biblical theology models.

E. Conclusion

The discussion offered by ancient Near Eastern scholars and the number of texts provided is quite impressive. Even if all the points of critique cannot be sustained, certainly their overall thesis appears quite convincing. Israel and the ancient Near East are quite similar in many respects concerning how the divine manifests itself in the affairs of people.

Many salvation history themes and motifs may be located among the ancient sources. Not only did the ancient world produce historiography comparable to Israel's, but similar themes of divine action, a divine plan, and the word of a deity bringing forth results may all be found in the ancient Near Eastern texts. This has led some critics to postulate that little or no difference may be found between Israel and the ancient Near East.[48] It is subjective and unfair of biblical theologians to deny historiographical capacity to Israel's contemporaries and then to ignore the textual evidence with all its analogies.

The best conclusion is provided by James Barr:

> . . . we should not place too much emphasis on the Israelite "God who acts in history" as a clear mark of a cultural distinctiveness which can also be directly evaluated theologically.[49]

Notes

1. Cancik, *Wahrheit, op. cit.*, p. 78; Porter, "Historiography," *op. cit.*, pp. 128–129; and Moshe Weinfeld, "Divine Intervention in War in Ancient Israel and in the Ancient Near East," *History, Historiography and Interpretation, op. cit.*, pp. 121–147.

2. Jacobsen, "Ancient Mesopotamian Religion: The Central Concerns," *Proceedings of the American Philosophical Society* 107 (1963): 479.

3. Albrektson, *History, op. cit.*, pp. 17–21.

4. Saggs, *Encounter, op. cit.*, pp. 81–88.

5. Albrektson, *History, op. cit.*, p. 67.

6. Translation in Kramer, "Sumerian Historiography," *Israel Exploration Journal* 3 (1953): 226.

7. Translation in James Pritchard, ed., *Ancient Near Eastern Texts Relating to the Old Testament,* 3rd ed. (Princeton, New Jersey: Princeton University, 1970), p. 458, lines 160–164, 168–169 (henceforth to be abbreviated as ANET), the full text of the lamentation is found in ANET 455–463.

8. Translation in Finkelstein, "The So-called 'Old Babylonian Kutha Legend,' " *Journal of Cuneiform Studies* 11 (1957): 85.

9. Translation in ANET 648–649, lines 62–65, 156–157, the complete text of the work is found in ANET 646–651; and Adam Falkenstein, "Fluch über Akkade," *Zeitschrift für Assyriologie* 57 (1965): 43–124, provided a complete text and a very thorough commentary on it.

10. Translation in ANET 354, lines 35–40, the complete text of the ritual is found in ANET 354–355.

11. Albrektson, *History, op. cit.,* p. 38.

12. *Ibid.,* p. 41.

13. Translation in Oliver Robert Gurney, *The Hittites* (Baltimore: Penguin, 1952), p. 174.

14. Translation of the prayer is found in ANET 395, paragraph 4.

15. Translation in Daniel Luckenbill, *Ancient Records of Assyria and Babylonia,* 2 vols. (New York: Greenwood, 1926), 1:61–62, paragraph 178.

16. Translation in Peter Machinist, "Literature as Politics: The Tukulti-Ninurta Epic and the Bible," *Catholic Biblical Quarterly* 38 (1976): 463, lines 36–39.

17. Translation in Albrektson, *History, op. cit.,* p. 22, who compared it to the Blessing of Isaac in Genesis 27:28–29 and Psalm 147:13–14. Cf. with the building inscriptions on the Temple of Anu and Adad which also contain very similar language and themes, text provided in Luckenbill, *Records, op. cit.,* pp. 97–100.

18. Translation in Albrektson, *History, op. cit.,* p. 20.

19. Translation in *ibid.,* p. 21.

20. Translation *in ibid.,* p. 32.

21. Lindblom, *Prophecy, op. cit.,* pp. 324–325.

22. Albrektson, *History, op. cit.,* pp. 34–35.

23. Ibid., pp. 42–49; and Saggs, *Encounter, op. cit.,* pp. 81–85.

24. Wyatt, "Observations," *op. cit.,* p. 829.

25. Albrektson, *History, op. cit.,* p. 27

26. Albrektson (*ibid.,* pp. 93–95) discussed the various ways in which the ancient Near Eastern worldview might be described as

cyclic: 1) The cycle of the year and the annual celebration of *akitu* festivities in Babylon was said to epitomize cyclic thought. Yet Albrektson found no trace of this festival's influence in historical literature. 2) Speiser, "Idea of History," *op. cit.*, p. 56; and Güterbock, "Tradition," *op. cit.*, pp. 113–115, said the ancient Near Eastern perception of the rise and fall of empires gave occasion to the development of a cyclic view of reality. But Albrektson noted this to be merely alternation in history rather than a true cyclic process. 3) It has been hypothesized that the ancients believed history would repeat the same events again some day. But no document affirms this belief either, according to Albrektson.

27. Gese, "Idea," *op. cit.*, pp. 59–60.
28. Saggs, *Assyria, op. cit.*, p. 126.
29. Machinist, "Tukulti-Ninurta," *op. cit.*, pp. 455–482.
30. Albrektson, *History, op. cit.*, pp. 90–93, 96, 110–111.
31. *Ibid.*, p. 93.
32. Saggs, *Encounter, op. cit.*, p. 83.
33. Albrektson, *History, op. cit.*, p. 95.
34. *Ibid.*, pp. 68–89.
35. *Ibid.*, p. 87.
36. Frederick Moriarity, "Word as Power in the Ancient Near East," *A Light unto My Path: Old Testament Studies in Honor of Jacob M. Myers,* Gettysburg Theological Studies, vol. 4, eds. Howard Bream, Ralph Heim, and Carey Moore (Philadelphia: Temple University, 1974), p. 359.
37. Albrektson, *History, op. cit.*, p. 67.
38. Kramer, *Sumerians, op. cit.*, p. 115; and Moriarity, "Word," *op. cit.*, pp. 346, 354.
39. Manfred Hutter, "Bemerkungen über das 'Word Gottes' bei den Hethitern," *Biblische Notizen* 28 (1985): 17–26.
40. John Wilson, "Egypt," *Before Philosophy,* ed. Henri Frankfort (Baltimore: Penguin, 1949), p. 60; and Moriarity, "Word," *op. cit.*, pp. 351–352.
41. Moriarity, "Word," *op. cit.*, p. 346.
42. Albrektson, *History, op. cit.*, p. 59, who also offered a number of examples (p. 55) as did Moriarity (*ibid.*, pp. 346–349, 353–359) which typify examples of a deity whose "word" brings about results in the realm of human affairs: 1) In the Sumerian account of the conflict between the cities of Umma and Lagash the "Word of Enlil" is said to have caused a net to be hurled upon the enemy in battle. 2)

The Sumerian king Entemena made a ditch according to the "Word of Enlil" and the "Word of Ningirsu." 3) The Sumerian king Urukagina of Lagash reformed the city around 2350 B.C. according to the "Word of Ningirsu." 4) The Sumerian city of Ur was defeated according to the Lament over the Destruction of Ur by the "Word of Enlil." The deity is especially praised for his power in this lament. 5) A Sumerian and Akkadian bilingual hymn to the god Nanna celebrates the power of his "Word." 6) In the Code of Hammurabi (1792–1750 B.C.) there is reference to the "potent Word of Enlil" which will cause violators of the law to be cursed. 7) Ammiditanna (1683–1647 B.C.) of Amorite Babylon speaks of the "Word of Ishtar" in a hymn of praise to her. 8) The Assyrian king Adad-Nirari I (1307–1275 B.C.) describes the intervention of various deities through a "powerful word" to destroy his enemies. 9) In the Apology of Hattushilis III or the Testament of Hattushilis III (1250 B.C.) the king perceives that the promised "Word of Ishtar" was fulfilled finally with his ascension to the throne. This promise and fulfillment pattern characterizes the epic literature in Genesis as well as the Deuteronomistic History. 10) The Assyrian king Ashur-resh-ishi I (1133–1116 B.C.) speaks of the "Word of Ninurta" to which he responds. 11) Nebuchadrezzar I (1124–1103 B.C.) of Kassite Babylon speaks of the "Word of Ishtar and Adad." 12) Tiglath-Pileser I (1115–1077 B.C.) of Assyria speaks in his annals of the "command" or "Word" of Ashur which directed his military campaigns. 13) In the text, Advice to a Prince, which comes from Babylon (1000–700 B.C.), the "Word of Enlil, Marduk, and Erra" are said to be able to bring punishment upon people. 14) In the Prism Inscription of Sennacherib (704–681 B.C.) of Assyria the "Word of Ashur" may bring the death of a king despite the decree of destiny. 15) In his Letter to the God the Assyrian king Esarhaddon (680–669 B.C.) speaks of the intervention of deities by a powerful "Word" to fight enemies. The inscription is quite similar to the earlier one of Adad-Nirari. 16) Ashurbanipal (668–627 B.C.) of Assyria speaks of the "Word of Ashur, Shamash, and Marduk" in his annals. 17) Chemosh, the god of Moab, orders king Mesha to fight Israel according to his "Word." And 18) the Canaanites had several terms for the "word of a deity," which include: *hwt, rgm,* and *tḥm.* Thus we find expressions like: "Your Word, O El, is wise," in *UT* 51, IV, 41: and "men may know your command," in *'NT* III, 23–25.

43. Albrektson, *History, op. cit.,* p. 122.
44. Moriarity, "Word," *op. cit.,* p. 345.

70

45. Albrektson, *History, op. cit.*, pp. 100–108.

46. *Ibid.*, p. 108.

47. *Ibid.*, p. 106.

48. Cancik, *Wahrheit, op. cit.*, pp. 72–76, and *Grundzüge, op. cit.*, p. 8; and Krecher and Müller, "Vergangenheitsinteresse," *op. cit.*, pp. 13–44.

49. Barr, *Old and New, op. cit.*, p. 72.

Chapter 6

Continuity of Basic Religious Values between Israel and the Ancient Near East

Critics of the biblical theologians' salvation history models also broadened their criticism to include some other aspects of comparison. They pointed to a number of similarities shared by Israel and the ancient Near East on basic religious values. The old dichotomy had portrayed the ancient world as cultic and ritualistic, while Israel moved in a moral and ethical direction. Critics stressed the "common theology" of Israel with the ancient Near East to mitigate against those stereotypes.

A. Similarity in Cultic Practices

Though cultic imagery at first consideration may have little to do with salvation history imagery, nonetheless the portrayal of this aspect of religious life had been a component of the biblical theologians' assessment. The linear perspective of Israel was said to have affected the cult and produced a more ethical perspective on reality. By way of contrast the ancient Near East lay steeped in magical, superstitious polytheism, divination, and a desire to manipulate the deities of the cosmos.

This stereotype received its due criticism. The contrast between ancient Near Eastern cult which was magical and

73

manipulative and the Israelite cult which emphasized freedom was overdrawn according to the critics. Ancient contemporaries of Israel did not seek to manipulate their gods any more than did Israelites. In both cultures people sought the good blessings which flowed from the deity/deities for this life and forgiveness of sins for a right relationship with that deity addressed by the petitioner. Babylonians implored the gods to act by offering sacrifices which the gods needed (biblical theologians would call this manipulation), but in Israel Yahweh was implored to act for the sake of praise and glory, for "his name's sake" in the Psalms (but this was not considered manipulative by biblical theologians). Critics saw very little difference in this distinction.[1]

The portrayal of god/gods in both cultures had more similarities than dissimilarities. The early portrayal of Yahweh cast him in the role of a typical Iron Age deity: he had a private name to be revealled to his devotees and it was kept secret for the sake of its inherent power, anthropomorphic images were attributed to the deity, he was accompanied in the heavens by an entourage—the *sebaoth* or "heavenly host," nature imagery was associated with the deity's person and actions, and he functioned as father, creator, judge, warrior, and king.[2] But biblical theologians either ignored or downplayed these early, crude images as poetic ways of describing God. In the later period the images associated with Yahweh were comparable to other theophoric descriptions found throughout the ancient world. Yahweh was portrayed like other ancient Near Eastern deities who were flattered in prayer as though they were the only deity in the heavens, even if the deity addressed were only a minor figure in the pantheon. Like other deities Yahweh was perceived as a personal being, described with anthropomorphic images, who was powerful but merciful in his total control of the realms of history, nature, and morality. In addition, like other deities he was bonded with a particular people for whom he cared and whose destinies he directed. This had been described as the "common theology" of the ancient world by various critics.[3] Even in his portrayal as the majestic creator of the universe by the exilic theologians Yahweh was still quite comparable to ancient deities like Ptah of Egypt and Marduk of Babylon.[4]

The worship of Yahweh reflected in the Psalms was said to be more personal, abstract, and sophisticated than ancient Near Eastern worship practices. But consideration of Mesopotamian cultic literature, especially from the later periods (first millennium B.C. in particular) again revealed great similarity between Israel and the neighboring cultures. The form and expressions used in the Psalms can be traced to Mesopotamian, especially Sumerian, hymns and petitionary "letter prayers." Further, in the Sumerian penitential hymns created in the first millennium B.C. the devotees began to ask for the removal of sin, not just the removal of the affliction resulting from sin. In this respect continuity with Israel's lament hymns may be observed. In fact, a structural relationship may be traced through the years of development. The early Mesopotamian city laments gave rise to a later genre of lament called *balag-eršemmas*, which appear to be the inspiration for biblical laments. One may even find Mesopotamian hymns with historical allusions, a characteristic expected to be unique to Israel. Mesopotamian hymns celebrating the rise of a dynasty or an empire are comparable to their biblical counterparts.[5]

Biblical theologians were accused of inconsistency in their evaluation of ancient divination. The ancient Near Eastern texts were chided for their mechanical deterministic prediction of future events. But later Babylonian texts were overlooked in this evaluation, for therein the determination of the divine will by investigating animal entrails, or extispicy, was dependent upon the free will of the gods to reveal truth to people.[6] By way of contrast the use of magic in the Hebrew Bible was described as being "broken" or having a "dialectical relationship" to real magic.[7] This, however, was also true in Babylon, for the *ašipu* priest spoke as an agent of the gods when he did incantations, he was not manipulating cosmic forces according to Babylonian understanding. In fact, Yahwism might be said to have many customs which appear equally magical in com-

75

parison to contemporaneous ancient Near Eastern activity, but biblical theologians downplayed these. Examples include the levitical purification laws, the power of the spoken word in blessings and curses, sacred lots, the custom of Azazel on Yom Kippur, and a number of reported incidents, such as Elisha and the arrows in II Kings 13:15–19.[8] Israel and the nations were all in a process of moving beyond the primitive magical perceptions of their primordial past.

Contrasts had been drawn between the determination of destinies in Babylon in the New Year festival, which implied a strong sense of fate, and the heavy emphasis in Israel upon human freedom and responsibility for individual and corporate actions. The ancient Near East supposedly decreed an impersonal fate for reality.[9] But critics affirmed that the decree of a polytheistic deity was no more impersonal than one by a monotheistic deity. Furthermore, Israel also believed in fate insomuch as God caused or created eternally ordained rituals, institutions, and natural phenomena, such as the Sabbath, the seasons, human marriage, and various aspects of the cult. Israel had divinely ordained, permanent institutions, so that one might say Israel too had a notion of fate and destiny comparable to Babylon.[10] Also, Mesopotamians saw activity among people on earth as independent and free at times, their actions not determined by pre-ordained patterns in the divine realm. Only if people were free by the understanding of the ancients would it be possible for the gods to become angered by the actions of people and kings. The dual reference to the will of the gods and the corresponding actions of people was no different than what occurs in biblical texts.[11]

Ancient Near Eastern specialists also objected to certain characterizations made of the ancient religions as being artificial, particularistic, and lacking in personal or private devotional dimensions. H. W. F. Saggs described quite well elements of the Babylonian religion to demonstrate that they had the religious elements of deep piety and personal commitment in the same measure as did Israelites. [12] The Babylonian cultus became no more artificial, moribund, alienating, or mechanistic than its Israelite counterpart could be at times. Saggs also criticized those who described Israel as the only people with a notion of universalism—a god who cares for all people everywhere—because as the only deity who existed all people came under his protection. Babylonian deities in polytheistic contexts could also love all people and have universal concerns.[13] Such universal love could also be attributed to Egyptian deities in hymns which moved in a monolatrous direction during the Late Kingdom period.[14]

Some biblical scholars have acknowledged Israel's indebtedness to the ancient world in terms of this personal perception of the deity. Israel's view of a personal deity, according to Gerald Janzen, was actually inherited from second millennium B.C. piety which had reacted against the older monarchical views of the gods in Mesopotamia. Personal religion developed in opposition to the third millennium B.C. nationalistic religion which viewed gods as leaders of individual city states. Gods were viewed as more gracious rather than warlike, concerned with individuals not the state. This personal religion was carried west to Israel where it became ultimately the religion of the entire population.[15]

B. Similarity of Social-Religious Perspectives

The stereotypes of biblical theologians had characterized Israel to be more linear, historical, ethical, moral, and even more modern than they actually were. Certain themes were emphasized while others were ignored in order to maintain this contrast. In the comparative examination of ancient Near Eastern and Israelite customs scholars often treated "true Israelite religion" as that of the reform oriented, prophetic and priestly leaders who brought monotheism and ethical-moral values to the people. All other religious expressions were due to syncretism with the surrounding culture and not truly Israelite, even though these other expressions seemed to be the property of the majority of the pre-exilic Israelite population according to the lament of the prophets. The prophetic Yah-wistic party was in the minority in the pre-exilic period and assumed the role of religious leadership only with the exile and post-exilic period. Comparing the values of this religious-political minority with the popular religious values of the ancient Near Eastern populace is unfair. It would be better to compare Israelite beliefs only with the highest and most moral expressions of religiosity taken from contemporary first millennium B.C. sources, for these alone would be the true equivalent to the Israelite sources. Often the biblical theologians described as typically ancient Near Eastern religious values those abuses attacked by the prophetic movement, which would hardly seek to portray the religious practices of opponents in a fair and objective fashion. In reality these "abuses" probably represented the typical, native Israelite religious practice of the pre-exilic period, which were attacked retrospectively by the later theological literature of the Yahwist party.[16]

Morton Smith and others have sought to describe a "common theology" of the ancient Near East which permeated Israel in equal measure as the other nations. If the religious practices of Israel were evaluated phenomenologically, the description of Israel's religion would differ little from that of the contemporary culture.[17] John Curtis noted that cyclic imagery was more extensive in the Hebrew Bible than is admitted by biblical theologians; it can be found in the "historical" patterns of the Yahwist (Genesis 2–11) and Deuteronomistic Historian, the festival cycle, the hope for a return to the Davidic or Messianic Age, and even in specific prophets like Hosea (return to the wilderness) and Deutero-Isaiah (the return will be a new creation and exodus).[18] The imagery of the "day of the Lord" is commonly found in Sumerian, Egyptian, Hittite, and Assyrian sources, and this was perceived by biblical theologians as a key concept connected to the matrix of ideas associated with divine action in history.[19] Israel inherited many ideas from the ancient Near East in matters of law, kingship, cult, and wisdom traditions.[20] Many more examples could be multiplied. John White listed a number of such areas wherein recent scholarship has obtained a better perspective of Israelite beliefs now that continuity between Israel and the ancient Near East has been acknowledged.[21]

Biblical theologians were led to contrast the two cultures because the impetus for this comparison lay in the biblical text itself. The Israelites in their theologized narratives and laws often tried to set themselves apart from the value systems of their ancient neighbors; the call to be different than the nations was a necessary ingredient in the self-identity for the preservation of the people of Yahweh. Classic examples of Israelite theological polemic against the nations include the Priestly hymn of creation in Genesis 1, the Yahwistic parody on Canaanite religion in Genesis 3, and prophetic attacks on the religious customs of other people found among the Israelites (especially Hosea, Jeremiah, and Ezekiel). Deutero-Isaiah most strongly attacked the belief in the existence of other gods and ridiculed the manufacture of sacred images. His critique was exaggerated, since the images used by the Babylonians were not seen by them as the divine reality, but rather an avenue of approach, like the Ark of the Covenant or the Temple.[22] The depth of critique offered by these Israelite spokespersons implied the need to create a distinct self-identity for the Yahwistic Israelites. This need was obviously magnified by the Babylonian exile, for at this point in their existence the Israelites faced amalgamation and extinction. Thus the need to create a separate identity and distance from the beliefs of the contemporary world has shaped the traditions in the Hebrew Bible to a great extent. Modern biblical theologians have been led by this theological agenda in the text to follow the lead of Yahwistic polemics and continue the stereotyping of ancient Near Eastern beliefs.

Israelite theologians called for social justice and by implication left their listeners and modern readers with the impression that the ancient world was devoid of justice. Idealistic visions of justice for all people and attempts at social reform can be found already in the third millennium B.C. in Mesopotamia and Egypt. The Israelites were heirs to a long tradition of social justice imagery. The notion that the king should defend the poor and the weak, bring justice to the whole land, and lead the people in gentleness and humility was an ideal which permeated the ancient world. They fell short of this ideal, of course, but so did kings in Judah and Israel.[23] Much of the imagery concerning this ideal king would find its way into the Psalms and prophetic literature of the Israelites.

Led by the tone of theological polemics in the text modern biblical theologians continued the contrast between Israelite and ancient Near Eastern beliefs and practices. This led to the creation of the historical-mythical paradigm as a tool for modern discussion. The result was an unfair evaluation which viewed the ancient world pejoratively in overemphasizing the primitive, while praising Israel unnecessarily for emphasizing the progressive. Critics responded by pointing out the sophistication in the contemporary cultures and the commonality Israel had with the ancient Near East.

Critics also sought to redefine the extent to which the linear salvation history perspective might be found in Israelite traditions. Scholars like Morton Smith who emphasized the concept of a "common theology" certainly limited the extent to which salvation history could be seen as Israel's unique theologomena. Others tried to deny its existence altogether. Bertil Albrektson attempted to discredit the notion by reducing the biblical testimony from the affirmation of a divine plan in history to a weaker concept of divine purpose. He even implied that the Assyrians had a more developed notion of divine action in history.[24] But this idea has not been received well by other scholars. H. W. F. Saggs has argued more cogently that salvation history really is present in the biblical text, but it means not so much the systematic activity of a deity in directing the affairs of all human history as the preservation of a particular religio-ethnic group called Israel. In reality this divine protection does not differ from what any other ancient Near Eastern deity in a polytheistic setting did for his or her own people.[25] Thus one may speak of Israel's salvation history perspective, but the conscientious scholar must admit the presence of this perspective already was developing among Israel's neighbors.

C. Conclusion

In conclusion ancient Near Eastern historians declared that Israel came into existence when the concept of a moral universe had been affirmed, the gods were perceived as acting in the social and historical realms as well as nature, social justice was possible in the divine-human relationship, and a collective and individual morality had developed.[26] Israel's religion was seen to be more closely connected to its ancient Near Eastern environment than biblical scholarship and been wont to admit. As a result some biblical scholars have begun to speak of Israel's close linkage with the religious thought of the ancient world. The best summary statement was provided by J. Roy Porter:

> . . . Israel formed part of the ancient Near Eastern world and it seems clear that many of the elements which help to make up the viewpoint and structure of Israelite historiography find their parallels in the surrounding civilizations, suggesting that Israel was heir to already established ideas of history and practices of history-writing.[27]

Notes

1. Roberts, "Cultic Manipulation," *op. cit.,* pp. 181–185.
2. Miller, "Israelite Religion," *op. cit.,* pp. 211–212.
3. Smith, "The Common Theology of the Ancient Near East," *Journal of Biblical Literature* 71 (1952): 135–147; and Norman Gottwald, "The Theological Task after The Tribes of Yahweh," *The Bible and Liberation: Political and Social Hermeneutics,* ed. Norman Gottwald (Maryknoll, New York: Orbis, 1983), p. 192.
4. Klaus Koch, "Wort und Einheit des Schöpfergottes in Memphis und Jerusalem," *Zeitschrift für Theologie und Kirche* 62 (1965): 251–293.

5. William Hallo, "Individual Prayer in Sumerian: The Continuity of a Tradition," *Essays in Memory of E. A. Speiser,* ed. William Hallo, American Oriental Series, vol. 53 (New Haven: American Oriental Society, 1968), pp. 71–89; Roberts, "The Religio-Political Setting of Psalm 47," *Bulletin of the American Schools of Oriental Research* 22 (1976): 132; and W. C. Gwaltney, "The Biblical Book of Lamentations in the Context of Near Eastern Lament Literature," *Scripture in Context II: More Essays on the Comparative Method,* eds. William Hallo, James Moyer, and Leo Perdue (Winona Lake, Indiana: Eisenbrauns, 1983), pp. 191–211.

6. Goetze, "An Old Babylonian Prayer of the Divination Priest," *Journal of Cuneiform Studies* 22 (1968): 25–29; and Roberts, "Cultic Manipulation," *op. cit.,* p. 187.

7. Fohrer, "Prophetie und Magie," *Zeitschrift für die alttestamentliche Wissenschaft* 78 (1966): 32, whose position was critiqued sternly by Roberts, "Cultic Manipulation," *op. cit.,* p. 186.

8. Roberts, "Cultic Manipulation," *op. cit.,* pp. 185–186.

9. Lambert, "Destiny," *op. cit.,* pp. 65–72.

10. Saggs, *Encounter, op. cit.,* pp. 70–76.

11. Roberts, "Myth Versus History," *op. cit.,* pp. 7–8.

12. Saggs, *Encounter, op. cit.,* pp. 153–175.

13. *Ibid.,* pp. 175–182.

14. Breasted, *Dawn, op. cit.,* pp. 276–289, and *Development of Religion and Thought in Ancient Egypt* (New York: Scribner's, 1912), pp. 315–331.

15. Gerald Janzen, "The Yoke That Gives Rest," *Interpretation* 41 (1987): 259–260.

16. Saggs, *Encounter, op. cit.,* pp. 21–26; and William Dever, "Material Remains and the Cult in Ancient Israel: An Essay in Archaeological Systematics," *The Word of the Lord Shall Go Forth: Essays in Honor of David Noel Freedman in Celebration of His Sixtieth Birthday,* eds. Carol Meyers and Michael O'Connor (Winona Lake, Indiana: Eisenbrauns, 1983), pp. 578–579.

17. Smith, "Common Theology," *op. cit.,* pp. 135–147, and "Religious Parties among the Israelites before 587," *Palestinian Parties and Politics That Shaped the Old Testament* (New York: Columbia University, 1971), pp. 15–56; and Gottwald, "Theological Task," *op. cit.,* p. 192.

18. Biggs, "Interpretation," *op. cit.,* pp. 115–123.

19. Douglas Stuart, "The Sovereign's Day of Conquest," *Essays*

in Honor of George Ernest Wright, eds. Edward Campbell and Robert Boling (Missoula, Montana: Scholars Press, 1976), pp. 159–164.

20. Reventlow, "Die Eigenart des Jahweglaubens als geschichtliches und theologisches Problem," *Kerygma und Dogma* 20 (1974): 201–208.

21. John White, "Universalization of History in Deutero-Isaiah," *Scripture in Context: Essays on the Comparative Method,* eds. Carl Evans, William Hallo, and John White, Pittsburg Theological Monograph Series, vol. 34 (Pittsburg: Pickwick, 1980), pp. 179–182, assessed the similarity between ancient Near Eastern values and the perspective of Deutero-Isaiah, pp. 179–192, after making the general observations noted in the text.

22. Saggs, *Assyria, op. cit.,* pp. 200–201, pointed out that Assyrian deities and their images were revered as symbolic; for example, the dagger could be seen as a symbol for Ashur, but the dagger would not be worshipped directly.

23. Breasted, *Development, op. cit.,* pp. 165–265, and *Dawn, op. cit.,* pp. 182–222; and Fensham, "Widow, Orphan, and the Poor," *op. cit.,* pp. 129–139.

24. Albrektson, *History, op. cit.,* pp. 68–69.

25. Saggs, *Encounter, op. cit.,* pp. 65–66.

26. Jacobsen, "Mesopotamian Religion," *op. cit.,* p. 484; and R. Rendtorff, "Die Entstehung der israelitischen Religion als religionsgeschichtliches und theologisches Problem," *Theologisches Literaturzeitung* 88 (1963): 746.

27. Porter, "Historiography," *op. cit.,* p. 127.

Chapter 7

The Continuing Debate over Israel's Concept of Salvation History

The scholarship and criticism provided by ancient Near Eastern historians has made an impression upon biblical studies. Some biblical scholars have concurred with these critiques and have moved their scholarship in a new direction which emphasizes continuity. Others, however, have reacted negatively to the work of Bertil Albrektson and others and have continued to defend the uniqueness of Israel's intellectual worldview.

A. More Balanced Perspective

If biblical scholars would move from their radical dichotomy of Israel and the ancient Near East, their understanding of Israel's thought and customs would benefit from a clearer perspective, so argue the critics. Biblical scholars overcharacterized the notion of salvation history, and this led them to unfair comparisons and the tendency to take Israelite and Near Eastern materials out of context.[1]

A number of biblical scholars have chosen a more balanced approach in comparative studies. German biblical scholars like Klaus Koch and Rolf Rendtorff, already in the last generation, began to emphasize the continuity of Israelite beliefs with the ancient Near Eastern milieu. Their approach was reminiscient of the old "history of religions" approach to Israelite materials, which had fallen into disrepute because of excessive

85

claims made by "history of religions" scholars prior to World War II.[2] The modern comparative method is more nuanced and has more ancient Near Eastern material at its disposal for consideration. Patrick Miller offered a good perspective for using the comparative method: acknowledge that Israel did consciously reject certain ideas from the surrounding world, but do not assume that silence on other issues should be taken as a rejection of commonly shared values.[3] In other words, assume divergence on Israel's part only when the Israelite theologians clearly make a claim or articulate a position that is truly different from contemporaneous belief.

This new comparative approach has yielded some valuable insight concerning Israelite faith and literature. Many of these observations have been in the theological-political arena. They are significant for our consideration because they result from the sympathetic study of ancient Near Eastern historiographical sources.

1) The literature in the books of Samuel concerning the rule of David reflects ancient Near Eastern ideology so well that scholars are induced to speak of an Apology of David, which may be embedded in the present narrative. Hittite and Assyrian apologies designed to legitimate the rise of a new king and his dynasty to the throne are particularly helpful in this comparison.[4] In another instance Abraham Malamat points out the similarities between Mursilis' Plague Prayer (1340–1310 B.C.) and David's treatment of the Gibeonites. Just as the Hittite king believed the plague was due to a treaty violation committed by his predecessor against Egypt, so the plague in David's reign was caused by Saul's treaty violation with Gibeon, a treaty established by Joshua. Hence, Saul's family had to be punished to expiate the plague.[5]

2) Ancient Near Eastern historiograpy provides us better insight into the Ark Narrative accounts in I Samuel 4–6 and II Samuel 6. The divine abandonment motif may be found in the Tukulti-Ninurta Epic and elsewhere. A deity may punish his or her people by leaving the sanctuary and dwelling among a foreign enemy, which then permits the defeat of the people in

battle. When the deity leaves this self-imposed exile and returns to his or her people, the punishment has been accomplished sufficiently to appease divine pride.[6] By placing I Samuel 1–3 with its account of the sins of the Elides before I Samuel 4–6 the loss of the Ark is seen as a result of Yahweh's anger against his own people, comparable to ancient Near Eastern versions.

3) Using kings from the distant past as paradigms for good and evil behavior which then brings appropriate blessing or punishment from the gods is well attested in ancient annals. Babylonian historiographers portrayed Sargon as good (though not always) and Naram-Sin as evil, and the latter defiled the sacred precincts of the Esagila and brought upon Akkad severe punishment according to Curse of Akkad, Cuthean Legend of Naram-Sin, and the Weidner Chronicle. Likewise in the Deuteronomistic History Jeroboam I of Israel was the archetypal evil ruler who deviated from the true worship at the Temple in Jerusalem, while David was the good king and archetype for the messianic ruler.[7] Furthermore, both literatures evaluate "history" in a theological perspective: how did rulers act toward the cult of the deity? This criterion was obviously anachronistic, since the cult became important only in later years. This was true not only with Jerusalem, for Josiah (621–609 B.C.) was the king who finally centralized worship in Jerusalem, but also in the Weidner Chronicle Naram-Sin is judged from the religious and cultic perspective of the later Kassite Babylonians of the second millennium B.C.[8]

4) Ancient Near Eastern historical sources often speak of the exile of a people and/or the destruction of their city as divine punishment in a way which reminds us vividly of Israel's theological reflections on the Babylonian exile. In the Prophetic Speech of Marduk the deity describes how he brought the defeat of his own people, then delivered them and rebuilt the city, which reminds us immediately of the language of Deutero-Isaiah. Esarhaddon of Assyrian and Cyrus of Persia speak of deities who returned scattered people to their homelands. Esarhaddon's report on Babylon and his reconstruction

of that city appear theologically oriented with clear religious perspectives; a religious explanation rather than historical narrative results. We are again reminded of the Deuteronomistic History.[9]

These few examples serve to illustrate the insights provided for biblical studies by ancient Near Eastern historiographical materials. As biblical theologians leave behind their stereotypes and the tendency to filter these ancient Near Eastern materials out of their research, scholarship on biblical narrative literature prospers.

B. The Unfolding Debate

The evidence provided by ancient Near Eastern scholars and historians did not go unchallenged, however. Biblical scholars and some ancient Near Eastern experts responded critically to the ideas raised by Bertil Albrektson and others. The result has been not only a debate which divides scholars, but a new and more sensitive understanding of Israel's relationship to the contemporary milieu may be developing.

Even as the *Heilsgeschichte* model was first articulated there were dissenting voices. In Germany Johannes Hempel noted that historical events as a form of divine action and especially as divine judgment might be perceived as a mode of viewing the gods in the rest of the ancient Near East.[10] In America early dissenters included Morton Smith who perceived that the prophetic-priestly tradition was only a segment of the pre-exilic faith and practice of Israel. In actuality, Israel had far more in common with the beliefs of ancient Near Eastern cultures. Smith spoke of the "common theology" held by Israel and the ancient world: All worshipped a god who was to be flattered in prayer as the only deity, even if he or she were a minor figure in the pantheon. This deity had power over the affairs of history, nature, and morality; he or she was merciful yet just, deserving love and fearful obedience from devotees, and granting rewards and punishments for human actions.[11]

These critics, however, were not regarded too seriously until later voices of protest critiqued the *Heilsgeschichte* models.

Among advocates of salvation history perspectives there were those with reservations. The most noted American proponent, George Ernest Wright, even observed that not all of the biblical materials fit the model. Wisdom Literature offered the chief difficulty in perceiving a common theology together with the historical and prophetic literature, for it lacked notions of history, election, and covenant.[12] Most significant were the reservations of Johannes Lindblom, a noted expositor of the uniqueness of the prophetic view of history. He observed a number of ancient Near Eastern parallels to the concept of salvation history, including the prologue to the Code of Hammurabi, the prayer of the Hittite king Telepinus, the Karnak Inscription of Tuthmosis III, the Mesha inscription from Moab, and an oracle given to the Assyrian king Esarhaddon.[13] Among the top scholars who advocated *Heilsgeschichte* models there was an awareness of the limitations.

Among German scholars a related debate arose concerning the significance of the figure of Moses in the biblical traditions. Martin Noth had virtually denied the existence of the historical personage Moses via traditio-historical investigation of texts in the Tetrateuch.[14] In the 1960's German scholars proceeded to deny the religious significance of Moses by declaring that no new religious insights and certainly no "religious revolution" could be traced to Moses, as William Albright had maintained in the 1940's. Rather the religion of Israel arose out of its ancient Near Eastern milieu; Moses did not found a new religion.[15] Klaus Koch and Rolf Rendtorff were criticized by Friedrich Baumgärtel for those views. Baumgärtel affirmed a significant discontinuity between Israel and the ancient Near Eastern environment.[16] But later scholarship has appeared to concur with Koch and Rendtorff.[17] Numerous German scholars have described Israel's religious odyssey as a slow development of monotheistic values, and concomitant with this they observe the essential continuity Israel had with the religious faith and practice of the ancient world.[18]

Substantial criticism arose in the English speaking world against *Heilsgeschichte* models in the 1960's. With the first edition of *Old and New in Interpretation* and other essays James Barr launched an insightful theological critique. From the ancient Near Eastern perspective Bertil Albrektson's *History and the Gods* was the most thorough analysis. By 1970 Brevard Childs could speak of the death of the Biblical Theology Movement and ideas like salvation history in his work, *Biblical Theology in Crisis.* The insights of these works have been discussed previously and need not be reviewed here.

Salvation history advocates rose to defend their pedagogical model against these criticisms, and the thesis of Albrektson was the chief target for rebuttal. Response was provided by scholars who did critical reviews of his work. Albrektson was criticized by Wilfrid Lambert, a noted Assyriologist whose views therefore commanded great respect, though Lambert agreed that biblical theologians had overstated their position and deserved criticism. Lambert agreed that the gods of the nations had control over both history and nature, but it was limited because polytheism created overlapping functions among various deities, and the gods still were rooted in natural forces and their place in the pantheon was determined by their descent from other deities. Mesopotamians could not have hypostatized the "Word" of a deity as did Israel who associated Yahweh's "Word" with his purpose and will. Lambert accused Albrektson of failing to understand Mesopotamian notions of destiny: the purported actions of the gods in history were really the unfolding of divinely determined destiny not history. These actions merely maintained the status quo rather than moving toward a goal. Furthermore, said Lambert, Albrektson's attempt to limit Israel's notion of salvation history by calling it divine purpose rather than a divine plan was simply "labored" and "inadequate."[19] C. J. Bleeker asserted that Albrektson underrated the importance of monotheism on Israel's values, thus the similarity he observed was outweighed by the dissimilarity ignored in his study.[20]

Contemporary with these reviews was the scholarship of J.

Roy Porter. He believed that the real answer lay between the extreme positions of the salvation history advocates and the Albrektson critique. He observed that though Hittite historiography was similar to that of the Israelites, the latter had far more developed narrative style. Porter felt that biblical material was closer in style to the later Islamic materials rather than to the earlier ancient Near Eastern sources. Israel was unique because of the integration of separate literary forms into one unified narrative. While the ancient Near East had the raw material for history, Israel provided a finished product which described that ethos of a whole people, the real life of everyday people.[21]

Paul Hanson tried to revive salvation history categories for use in theological discussion.[22] Hanson rejected Albrektson's attempt to deny the idea of a plan in Israel's epic materials. In particular, Hanson turned to Jewish apocalyptic as a model of Jewish understanding of history, and he attempted to restate the salvation history model by observing the development of historiography from the prophetic to apocalyptic genres. In so doing, he contrasted Israelite historiography with ancient Near Eastern models.[23] Mesopotamian sources could not be termed "history," for they lacked "historical sequence spanning centuries in an unbroken development," and in "reflecting cosmic events" they were "reflecting timeless episodes." This was quite different than the materials in the Hebrew Bible.[24]

In the 1970's J. J. M. Roberts also criticized the *Heilsgeschichte* approach, especially that of George Ernest Wright, and he affirmed the work of Albrektson against critics like Lambert and Hanson. He also applauded the insights of James Barr and Brevard Childs. Wright was criticized for establishing a comparison between Israel and early Mesopotamian materials rather than using the later Mesopotamian sources, for this enabled Wright to highlight the contrast between Israel and the ancient world.[25] In other articles Roberts criticized Lambert and Hanson for their evaluation of Albrektson. He pointed to work by Kirk Grayson on Assyrian inscriptions and the Babylonian Chronicles which proved that these materials did not arise out of Mesopotamian divination as Lambert had claimed. Roberts attacked Hanson's characterization of Mesopotamian historiography as timeless, cosmic, and mythic. He rejected Hanson's comparison of biblical and ancient Near Eastern historiography, for in Roberts' view the method of the Deuteronomistic Historian differed little from contemporary counterparts: both placed pre-existing blocks of literary material together in disparate fashion. But Roberts did admit differences existed; more sensitive comparisons between Israel and the ancient Near East were required in his opinion.[26] In another article Roberts endeavored to give a more careful and sensitive analysis of ancient Near Eastern reports by Nebuchadnezzar I as illustrative of this newer procedure.[27]

At the same time other scholars began to make similar observations. Robert Drews sensed that the consensus was moving toward a more favorable consideration of ancient Near Eastern texts.[28] Patrick Miller and Roberts produced an assessment of the Ark Narrative in the books of Samuel which demonstrated continuity with ancient Near Eastern historiography, thus providing another example of the use of ancient Near Eastern historiographical sources in a positive fashion to enlighten our understanding of biblical texts.[29]

In recent years two very significant works have been produced. In 1978 H. W. F. Saggs provided scholars with his book, *The Encounter with the Divine in Mesopotamia and Israel*. Herein he compared notions of history, good and evil, personal piety, universalism, and the idea of God in Mesopotamia and Israel. He found a great deal of similarity, and he criticized biblical theologians who forced comparisons in order to affirm Israel's uniqueness. His work was broader in scope and more phenomenological in approach than Albrektson's, but it reinforced the earlier work quite well.[30] In 1984 Jan Van Seters wrote a thorough evaluation of ancient Near Eastern and biblical historiography. He affirmed the critiques of Albrektson and Roberts in particular.[31] He portrayed biblical historiography as contemporaneous with Greek historians and as building upon a well developed tradition of ancient Near

Eastern historiography.[32] Together these two works offered a wealth of comparative material critical of the biblical theologians and their *Heilsgeschichte* models.

Recently some authors have tried to revive the salvation history perspective. From a general theological perspective Werner Lemke sought to defend Wright's approach. Lemke widened the definition of salvation history to mean "events," rather than history, so that the term would be broad enough to apprehend revelation by "words" as well as "deeds." In so doing, he sought to respond primarily to the theological critique of James Barr and others. The literature of the Bible contains both objective facts and subjective perceptions or interpretations of the events, so both should be called salvation history.History is a philosophical category, event is more an authentic biblical category; and critics of the salvation history paradigm had attacked defenders as though they spoke of the former when they really intended the latter meaning.[33] Lemke's position recognized and responded to the theological critique, but really did not seek to reaffirm Israel's uniqueness in the face of ancient Near Eastern critics.

From a historiographical perspective Joseph Licht sought to defend the uniqueness of Israel's historical perspective. He criticized Mesopotamian materials as being merely annals, and more importantly as being only accounts of short periods of time and records of recent events rather than the distant past. Like Lambert he believed that Albrektson and Saggs confused Mesopotamian ideas of "destiny" with the Israelite notion of "history." Israel's deity had a deliberate, "long term policy" over successive generations for future events and no ancient Near Eastern text had that.[34] (However, he did not admit that some of the Babylonian materials reviewed periods of time longer than the entire biblical era.)

In a very general essay Benjamin Uffenheimer sought to evaluate Israel in social-historical categories. When surveying Israel's contributions to the "axial age," he relied heavily upon the old models of cyclic myth and linear epic history and the observations derived from those categories.[35] Since his sources were dated, he did not actually engage in the ongoing debate, but his work exemplified the introduction of social-historical categories into an already complex debate.

C. Conclusion

Thus it seems that in the debate which has been raised for the past twenty-five years the tide of victory may belong to the critics of salvation history paradigms. The works of Albrektson, Saggs, and Van Seters remain as monuments to be reckoned with. But a very important nuance must be sounded. These critics do not seek to remove all pedagogical discussion of comparison between Israel and the ancient Near East. They do not wish to reduce Israel to being just another ancient Near Eastern culture. They perceive that Israel was different in some regard and that something was created which became a cornerstone of western civilization. What they seek is a more sensitive comparison which is accurate in its discussion of Israelite beliefs and not unfair in its description of the ancient Near East. They have cleared the ground for a more sensitive and nuanced portrayal of salvation history. We are ready to move to a third stage of the modern discussion.

Notes

1. Westermann, "Grenze," *op. cit.,* pp. 489–496; and Saggs, *Encounter, op. cit.,* pp. 1–29.

2. Klaus Koch, "Der Tod der Religionsstifters," *Kerygma und Dogma* 8 (1962): 100–123; R. Rendtorff, "Entstehung," pp. 735–746, and "Mose als Religionsstifter?," *Gesammelte Studien zum Alten Testament* (Munich: n.p., 1975), pp. 152–171.

3. Miller, "Israelite Religion," *op. cit.,* p. 211.

4. Wolf, "Apology of Hattushilis," *op. cit.,* passim; Roberts, "The Ancient Near Eastern Environment," *Hebrew Bible, op. cit.,* p. 88; Cancik, *Wahrheit, op. cit.,* pp. 61–64; Tadmor, "Apology," *op. cit.,* pp. 36–57, referred to the Assyrian apologies of Shamshi-Adad V (824–811 B.C.), Esarhaddon (680–669 B.C.), and Ashurbanipal (669–

627 B.C.); and Kyle McCarter, *I Samuel,* The Anchor Bible (Garden City, New York: Doubleday, 1980), pp. 27–30.

    5. Malamat, "Causality," *op. cit.,* pp. 1–12.

    6. Machinist, "Tukulti-Ninurta," *op. cit.,* pp. 462–464; and Miller and Roberts, *The Hand of the Lord: A Reassessment of the "Ark Narrative" of 1 Samuel,* The Johns Hopkins Near Eastern Studies, ed. Hans Goedicke (Baltimore: Johns Hopkins University, 1977), pp. 9–17, 69–75.

    7. Osswald, "Parallelen," *op. cit.,* pp. 266–296; and Carl Evans, "Naram-Sin and Jeroboam: The Archetypal Unheilsherrscher in Mesopotamian and Biblical Historiography," *Scripture in Context II, op. cit.,* pp. 97–125.

    8. Osswald, "Parallelen," *op. cit.,* pp. 288–293; and Evans, "Naram-Sin," *op. cit.,* pp. 108, 121.

    9. J. A. Brinkman, "Through a Glass Darkly: Esarhaddon's Retrospects on the Downfall of Babylon," *Journal of the American Oriental Society* 103 (1983): 41; Robert McFadden, "Micah and the Problem of Continuities and Discontinuities in Prophecy," *Scripture in Context II, op. cit.,* p. 144; and George Widengren, "Yahweh's Gathering of the Dispersed," *In The Shelter of Elyon: Essays on Ancient Palestinian Life and Literature in Honor of Gösta W. Ahlström,* eds. Boyd Barrick and John Spencer, Journal for the Study of the Old Testament Supplement Series, vol. 31 (Sheffield, England: JSOT Press, 1984), pp. 227–245.

    10. Johannes Hempel, *Altes Testament und Geschichte,* Studien des apologetischen Seminars, vol. 27 (Gütersloh: n.p., 1930), pp. 9–11, and *Geschichten und Geschichte im Alten Testament bis zur persischen Zeit* (Gütersloh: n.p., 1964), pp. 86–88.

    11. Smith, "Common Theology," *op. cit.,* pp. 135–147, and "Religious Parties," *op. cit.,* 15–56.

    12. Wright, *God Who Acts, op. cit.,* p. 103.

    13. Lindblom, *Prophecy, op. cit.,* pp. 324–325. The texts may be read in *ANET,* pp. 165, 270, 320, 374, 397.

    14. Noth, *A History of Pentateuchal Traditions,* trans. Bernhard Anderson (Englewood Cliffs, New Jersey: Prentice-Hall, 1972), pp. 156–175.

    15. Koch, "Tod," *op.cit.,* pp. 100–123; R. Rendtorff, "Entstehung," *op. cit.,* pp. 735–746, and "Mose," *op. cit.,* pp. 152–171. Their position was in opposition to that of William Albright, *From the Stone Age to Christianity: Monotheism and the Historical Process* (Baltimore: Johns Hopkins University, 1940), pp. 1–403.

16. Friedrich Baumgärtel, "Der Tod des Religionsstifters," *Kerygma und Dogma* 9 (1963): 223–233.

17. Fritz Stolz, "Monotheismus in Israel," *Monotheismus, op. cit.*, pp. 174–175.

18. See the essays in Keel, ed. *Monotheismus, op. cit.*, pp. 12–184; and Bernhard Lang, ed., *Der einzige Gott: Die Geburt des biblischen Monotheismus*, (Munich: Kösel, 1981), pp. 9–113.

19. Lambert, "A Review," *op. cit.*, pp. 170–177, and "Destiny," *op. cit.*, pp. 65–72.

20. C. J. Bleeker, "Review of Bertil Albrektson, History and the God," *Bibliotheca Orientalis* 26 (1969): 229.

21. Porter, "Pre-Islamic Arabic Historical Traditions and the Early Historical Narratives of the Old Testament," *Journal of Biblical Literature* 87 (1968): 17–26, and "Historiography," *op. cit.*, pp. 130–131.

22. Paul Hanson, *Dynamic Transcendence* (Philadelphia: Fortress, 1978), pp. 23–60.

23. *Idem.*, "Jewish Apocalyptic Against Its Near Eastern Environment," *Revue biblique* 78 (1971): 31–58.

24. *Ibid.*, p. 38.

25. Roberts, "Cultic Manipulation," *op. cit.*, pp. 181–187.

26. *Idem.*, "Myth Versus History," *op. cit.*, pp. 1–13, and "Environment," *op. cit.*, p. 88.

27. *Idem.*, "Elamite Crisis," *op. cit.*, pp. 183–187.

28. Drews, "Sargon," *op. cit.*, p. 387.

29. Miller and Roberts, *Hand of the Lord, op. cit.*, pp. 1–17.

30. Saggs, *Encounter, op. cit.*, pp. 1–188.

31. Van Seters, *History, op. cit.*, pp. 57–59.

32. *Ibid.*, pp. 1–362.

33. Werner Lemke, "Revelation through History in Recent Biblical Theology," *Interpretation* 36 (1982): 34–46.

34. Joseph Licht, "Biblical Historicism," *History, Historiography and Interpretation, op. cit.*, pp. 109–111.

35. Benjamin Uffenheimer, "Myth and Reality in Ancient Israel," *Axial Age, op. cit.*, pp. 135–168.

Chapter 8
Reconstruction of a Salvation History Model

Despite the great debate between scholars the fact remains that the Hebrew Scriptures still contain a large portion of narrative or historical literature, more extensive than is found in the ancient Near East. This alone demands the continued discussion of the nature of "salvation history" as a theologomena in describing biblical materials. What remains is to apprehend this model in a more nuanced fashion so as to accurately describe Israel's perceptions in relationship to the rest of the ancient world. Having accomplished this the new model may be of service to biblical theology.

If scholars are to speak of salvation history in a meaningful fashion they must come to grips with the ancient Near Eastern material more seriously. No longer will they so radically contrast Israel with the nations. The degree to which Israel is different will be more carefully defined and future reference to those issues of divergence ought to be more precise in future scholarship and pedagogical writings.

A new reconsideration of *Heilsgeschichte* paradigms might select any one of several modes for describing the degree to which Israel's values differed from those of neighboring cultures. Scholars may choose to speak of a basic continuity between Israelite views and those of the ancient Near East, or they may prefer to speak of basic similarity with only a slight degree of difference overall, or scholars may emphasize one particular aspect or key ingredient in the matrix of Israelite belief which appears to be the point of divergence.

The scholars who engage in the debate concerning the nature of salvation history models, especially those critical of biblical theologians, often suggest helpful insights which will serve as points for departure in this discussion. This chapter shall review some of those suggestions to see which ones might have value for reconstructing a salvation history model and describing Israel's significant ideational contributions.

A. Continuity

Some scholars affirm that with the notion of Yahweh acting in human events Israel was no different than neighboring societies, and perhaps this similarity could be extended to other particulars of Israel's religious experience. One might concur with Rolf Rendtorff when he said:

> The revelation of God in the history of Israel and in its religion is indissolubly linked with the history and religious history of the ancient Near East.[1]

Likewise Jon Levenson strongly observed that searching for something unique in Israelite beliefs was a "wild goose chase," for everything Israelite ultimately had a non-Israelite origin.[2] Morton Smith moved in this direction with his observations. For him the prophetic-priestly tradition which produced our present text was not, properly speaking, the real pre-exilic Israel. They were a minority whose views came into general acceptance only during the exile, whereas the faith and practice of early Israel had much in common with the rest of the ancient world.[3] Thus Israel would be seen as being no different than neighboring cultures in viewing the action of the deity/deities in history. Yet he does recognize that the views of this prophetic-priestly minority were truly different than those of the contemporary world. Even if they were a minority in the pre-exilic period, their values would be worth evaluating in contrast to prevalent religious and social views of the surrounding milieu. So let us admit that Yahwists were in the minority in pre-exilic Israel, but then ask the comparative question of their particular views.

A number of scholars have likewise emphasized Israel's strong religious continuity with the surrounding cultures. Pedagogically they preferred to reject the notion of Israel's uniqueness in order to more accurately describe Israelite religion.[4] Though they have rejected the paradigm which places Israel in opposition to the ancient Near East, in their writings they have described the Israelite faith on its own terms. One might then move from their suggestions to engage in a more nuanced comparative method. In this endeavor the "comparative approach must recognize the continuity between Israelite Yahwism and the religions of Canaan and Mesopotamia."[5]

The explanation for Israel's continuity would be found in their historical experience. Not only were they encircled and obviously influenced by other cultures, their origin was in the lands of Egypt and Canaan. Many Israelites were formerly Canaanites who "switched sides" either by peaceful withdrawal or by revolution. We concur with Gösta Ahlström that:

> Although the people abandoned the Canaanite societies, they took with them the culture and religion which they had always known and retained them in their new settlements.[6]

In reality many scholars who have spoken of the great similarity between Israel and the ancient Near East were reacting against those who overemphasized the contrasts. Closer inspection reveals that they would differentiate the beliefs in some way, just as one would differentiate Hittite, Babylonian, Assyrian, and Egyptian belief-systems from each other. Israelite ideas would belong in a general discussion with these other cultures, but there would be some identifying characteristics peculiar to Israelite faith and practice.

B. Degree of Difference

Most critics of salvation history models would prefer to say that Israel had the same values as neighboring cultures but the difference was a matter of degree not antithesis. A typical expression would be the statement by James Barr that certain elements "differ in degree, in pattern and in relation," but they do not "differ absolutely" nor are they "capable of univocal theological evaluation."[7]

Most helpful are the observations of J. J. M. Roberts who perceived that though there was a basic similarity between Israel and the ancient Near East, one might speak in nuanced terms of Israel's own particular identity. Both Israel and the ancient world used the same literary technique in historiography and had the understanding of human freedom and responsibility in the face of the divine realm at times.[8] When biblical theologians described the ancient Near Eastern religions as a-historical and manipulative in the cultic arena, he admitted that there was some truth in this regard. While Mesopotamians and Israelites both celebrated historical events in their respective cults, the Mesopotamians were more pervasive in translating historical events into the cosmic language of myth. "It is more difficult to find Mesopotamian religious texts that speak of historical events in non-mythological language."[9] Roberts would concede a "relative superiority to the Israelite works," but he would remind us quickly that Mesopotamians had a historiography which "saw a continuity is history."[10] Roberts has provided some of the more concrete suggestions for future discussion.

In similar fashion John Hayes has observed that Israel's greater emphasis upon salvation history imagery resulted from their late appearance in the ancient Near East. They came into existence after the Bronze Age had ended with the rise of the Iron Age. Because of their late appearance they used the historiographical style of writing more earnestly as a mode of discourse after the predecessor cultures had initiated and developed it.[11]

Klaus Koch and Graf Reventlow pointed out the central aspect of Israel's thought was the emphasis upon human freedom and responsibility with a non-cultic perspective of divine action in human affairs. These ideas were not unique to

100

Israel, but they were emphasized in Israel to a greater degree than elsewhere. Continuity rather than divergence was the way these scholars perceived the relationship.[12] However, one might take their observations and prefer to speak of these aspects as the issue on which Israel exhibited a significant degree of departure from the rest of the ancient world rather than describing the process as simple continuity.

Bertil Albrektson admitted there were nuances of difference. Divine purpose, for example, must be conceived differently in polytheistic religions, for Hebrew religion with its monotheism would not allow any rival plans in the divine realm or conflicting divine actions. In Israel there was a tendency toward a "unitary perspective of history." Also this perspective would view a longer period of time and have a more distant aim for divine actions, but Albrektson considers this a difference of degree not conceptual divergence. Finally, Israel's cult was historicized to a greater extent, for it concentrated on the great acts of God, and so festivals were historicized. Nowhere else in the ancient world were saving acts in history so central in the cult, where they dominated in the great festivals held throughout the year.[13]

In a social historical study of Israel's origins Gösta Ahlström made comparable observations about Israel's material culture in general. Though Israel withdrew from Canaanite environs and retained the same material cultural practice and values, their continued hostility with Canaanite urban centers and the resulting desire to diverge from those old cultural practices led to a number of consistent re-adaptations of the Canaanite values.[14]

Finally, this position may only be one step away from saying that Israel was indeed different, but only in regard to one or two central ideological issues. In that case some of our scholars might be very close to the position to be described below.

C. Particular Points of Divergence

The avenue of approach preferred by a majority of scholars is to emphasize a central theme or idea, crucial to the matrix of Israelite values and focus upon it as Israel's unique point of departure from contemporary values. Particular aspects are highlighted by some ardent defenders of the old salvation history models as well as by critics of those models who seek a more nuanced perspective in assessing Israel. This way of approaching the issue could be the compromise position amenable to most scholars involved in the debate. Occasionally scholars from both sides in the debate discuss one particular theme as a starting point for stressing Israel's contributions. This indicates that proponents of both sides in the debate are not removed so totally from the other position, rather the debate is a matter of perspective and emphasis.

To select for discussion certain themes and use these as points of departure in biblical theology is an advance over previous salvation history paradigms. For previously sweeping generalizations were made that simply were not true in regard to the evaluation of biblical and ancient Near Eastern values. Such an approach is the more sensitive and nuanced procedure called for in the discussion.

When engaging in this process the scholar must be circumspect in regard to precise clarification of the particular theologomena. One must not overlook ancient Near Eastern parallels, nor create an abstraction actually unknown to Israel, nor read too much into the various texts. As Moriarity stated: "But uniqueness must not be purchased at the price of distinctions which cannot be supported in the texts."[15] The following notions are among those used by scholars as possible ways in which Israel departed from the ancient Near Eastern worldview:

1. Total Freedom from Nature Imagery

Some would declare that Israel went beyond other cultures by placing Yahweh above the forces of nature in a radical way not possible in the polytheistic settings of ancient Near Eastern religions. Though ancient Near Eastern imagery concerning the gods had become social and anthropomorphic by the first millennium B.C., nonetheless, the earlier nature imagery remained. Even George Ernest Wright admitted that metaphors surrounding deities like Baal and Enlil had moved from the natural realm to the social realm with images of king, lord, parent, judge, warrior, and craftsman, but he maintained that the gods "never shook off their primary relation to the storm" and they were "imposed on the earlier forms." With Yahweh, however, social metaphors were borrowed from neighboring religions, and they were not imposed upon pre-existing nature images, for Yahweh's primary arena of apprehension had been the great acts associated with the Exodus.[16]

Other authors in addition to Wright have pursued this same line of argument. Georg Fohrer emphasized that Israelite religion portrayed a deity who acted directly and personally in an ethical mode rather than through the forces of nature. Israel still viewed Yahweh as a god over the forces of nature, but the new nuance placed less emphasis on nature as a mode of divine communication.[17] Wilfrid Lambert likewise asserted that the social imagery surrounding the deities of the ancient Near East was limited, not only because of their roots in natural forces but also because they had fixed places in the pantheon and a divine lineage, descent from other deities. An ancient Near Eastern god could never transcend his or her limitations of being one deity among many with clear connections to particular functions in the divine realm and the phenomena of nature, while Yahweh was free from all these inhibiting features.[18] Yahweh was unique in that Israelites refused to identify him with natural phenomena and subsequently prohibited any images of him. Saggs found this to be the uniqueness of Yahweh, and he described it as the "recognition of what God was not."[19]

The observations of these scholars imply that if Yahweh was more removed from the nature imagery found among contemporary deities in the surrounding milieu, then one might speak of Yahweh's action in the arena of history as being relatively more conspicuous in his theophoric attributes. Such a conclusion may indeed be the case, but it is difficult to really call this a true divergence from the ancient Near Eastern beliefs. The first millennium B.C. views held by Mesopotamians and others were moving in this direction already; Israel simply continued a developmental process already established. Furthermore, to isolate this facet may lead scholars to ignore the strong nature imagery used to describe the theophanies of Yahweh in the early literature, especially the poetry. Such strong nature imagery is used of Yahweh, especially when he is described as the divine warrior; it then would be inappropriate to say that Israel moved significantly beyond contemporary societies in this regard. What we may have is not really the point of departure from ancient Near Eastern values, nor something unique to Israel, but a way in which Israelite thought continued the evolutionary advance already in process.

2. Total Affirmation of History as the Arena for Divine Activity

Another approach similar to the previous perspective would go farther in describing Yahweh's behavior as operative in the arena of human history. Though it would refrain from drawing all of the conclusions of the old linear and cyclic comparisons, nonetheless, it would accept the starting point of old *Heilsgeschichte* models as correct. It would assign to Israelite religion the rather bold stroke of perceiving Yahweh to be totally a god of historical activity. While admitting that ancient Near Eastern deities intervened in human affairs (unlike the older salvation history models did), advocates would maintain that Israel went significantly beyond contemporary perceptions. The mere intervention of a deity in human affairs is not truly salvation history as found in Israel's description of Yahweh's behavior. Bertil Albrektson minimized the depth of Israel's understanding of salvation history by interpreting the texts to affirm merely divine purpose rather than divine plan. Few would agree with him so far as to say that Israel's views of divine action in history were really no different than those of the Mesopotamians. Most scholars would consider Israel's

104

views qualitatively different, and some believe this to be the starting point for a discussion of Israel's theological contributions.

Herbert Butterfield characterized this viewpoint the best. He saw that the ancient Near East had a notion of the gods executing judgment in history by punishing governments for their sins with various disasters, but Israel believed that all history was based on a grand divine promise, and they were "more obsessed by history than any other, either before or since."[20] Of the ancient Near East he said: "It would be wrong to deny such interest, but it might also be imprudent to attach too much importance to it."[21] He could conclude:

> . . . the tradition which came to dominate in Israel attached itself to the God of History rather than the God of nature. The Yahweh who brought his children out of the land of Egypt seemed to matter more than even the Yahweh who created the world.[22]

More recent scholarship has resonated similar notions concerning Israel's heavy emphasis upon history in contrast to neighboring societies. Robert Drews noted: ". . . there is little evidence that the Mesopotamian public knew much or cared much about history."[23] Paul Hanson attempted to see a developmental process wherein there gradually arose a greater stress upon history as a mode of divine behavior. In early mythology history was negated, but in Mesopotamian literature history existed if only as a reflection of activity in the divine realm. In Israel's early historiography myth and history stood in tension with each other, but with prophetic theology history was affirmed as the ultimate arena of divine behavior. With the rise of apocalyptic literature there came an indifference to historical restraints, and finally gnostic thought negated the historical realm altogether. Thus Israel produced those only moments wherein history was perceived with great clarifty as the realm of divine actions.[24] Finally, James Barr admitted:

> . . . there really is a Heilsgeschichte, a series of events set within the plan of human life and in historical sequence, through which

God has specially revealled himself . . . . this can be taken as the central theme of the Bible, that it forms the main link between Old and New Testaments, and that its presence and importance clearly marks the biblical faith off from other religions.[25]

As with the first position these arguments and insights are valuable for consideration. However, to say that Israel radically affirmed history as the arena for divine behavior might lend itself to overgeneralization, and the authentic nature imagery associated with Yahweh might be relegated to an insignificant role in the discussion of biblical theology. None of the above mentioned scholars would be guilty of that, to be sure, but were the discussion to move in this direction, such a biased viewpoint could develop. It would be best to say again that Israel moved further in this direction than contemporary cultures, but that movement had already been established before Israel's appearance. Israel is not unique in this regard, rather an intellectual developmental process was given great impetus by creative Israelite theologians.

3. Divine Actions in History Denote Purpose

A different emphasis might seek to contrast the purpose of divine actions in the ancient Near East and in Israel. While in the ancient world the gods merely punished kings and nations for cultic offenses, Yahweh had a purpose behind his direction that had implications for the future. The former would be divine "maintenance" whereas the latter would imply divine "process."

Wilfrid Lambert perceived that Mesopotamian deities intervened only to maintain certain cultic norms, they were angered by sacrilege of their sacred shrines by the kings. When they punished kings and countries they did so in order to uphold the cultic status quo rather than to move toward some ultimate and new religious goal. The Babylonian notion of destiny implied just such a legitimation of traditional social norms with an annual re-establishment at the New Year festival. The idea of destiny assumes the notion of status quo and maintenance, not a general plan in history, said Lambert. Destruction by a deity was always temporary, and eventually that city would return to its glory and the favor of the gods some day. There ultimately was no real change. Yahweh, however, worked with greater purpose in his plan for the historical arena. Often the message of divine spokespersons called for some social and religious change, the notion of a return to the status quo was not found here.[26]

One might criticize this from several angles. Bertil Albrektson, for example, would prefer to describe Israel's view as one of "divine purpose" rather than a "divine plan" in regard to Yahweh's future intentions, and this supposedly differed little from Mesopotamian beliefs.[27] He has found little support for his arguments, however. One might critically suggest that Israel's call to reform, especially among the prophets, was really an attempt to return to an earlier age, hence a desire to return to an earlier status quo. Likewise, the future hope of a messianic age was an attempt to relive the age of David, and the messiah was to be a *'David redivivus'* or a "new David." But these arguments might be a little labored, since any call for progress or change will use poetic imagery and inspirational metaphors of past ages. Movements of social change usually need to legitimate authentic progress by showing how their roots are found in traditional values worth emulating.

If indeed, Israel's beliefs include the notion of divine purpose and change in the human sphere, this is a significant departure from previous thought in the ancient world. This notion will be significant in future discussions of biblical theology and Israel's peculiar contributions to intellectual development.

4. Long Range Purpose or Plan in History

A variation on the previous argument would place the unique Israelite emphasis on the notion of Yahweh's long-range plans for Israel. This argument would admit that ancient Near Eastern deities acted purposively in history (if only to maintain the status quo), but the essential difference was that the Israelites

107

believed all the actions of Yahweh fit together into a grand scheme. The actions of ancient Near Eastern deities would be seen as isolated responses repeated because of similar cultic offenses, but Yahweh had a grand vision for the people of Israel.

Several scholars have used this comparison in their discussions. Herbert Butterfield implied this point of view when he described Israel's history as unified under the notion of promise and fulfillment, a motif he found discussed by biblical theologians. While the Mesopotamians may have preceded the Yahwist epic historian in writing a grand account of human history over a long period of time, the priests of Marduk lacked the Yahwist's over-arching theme of promise and fulfillment, which went from patriarchal material down to the monarchy. Only the Hebrew Bible had such a "large-scale interpretation." The priests of Babylon or the Hittite account of Telepinus put together episodes to show how disasters fell on monarchs or how dynasties were legitimated, but the result was far from being the history of a country or a people. Israel alone provided such a grand account.[28] Johannes Lindblom attributed this grand vision of history to the prophetic theologians:

> . . . the prophets regarded the history of Israel as a coherent history directed by moral principles and in accordance with a fixed plan . . . other ancient peoples had nothing corresponding to this view of history . . . as the realization of a fixed plan from its beginning to its end is to be found elsewhere in the ancient world.[29]

Joseph Licht stated that while Mesopotamia produced "records of recent events" rather than the distant past, Israel envisioned divine actions as a "deliberate long-term policy."[30] From a totally different perspective J. Roy Porter has suggested that Israel developed a consciousness of a long range plan in history because of the consciousness of past "successive stages of development in the growth of Israel." This consciousness gave rise to real historiography.[31] Israelites

108

were "latecomers" to ancient Near Eastern society; they could not trace their origins back to the beginning of time as was done in the great river civilizations, and their origins were outside of the land in which they resided. They were conscious of their origin as an event within human memory. Hence, history arose as the result of reflection upon events in the lives of normal people.[32]

Most recently writers have sought to articulate more precisely the distinction that Israel's view of history had a long range goal without denying that the ancient Near East appears to have had a notion of a grand divine purpose or plan in history. They emphasize the fact that a goal implies change, while a plan may imply only stasis. Hartmut Gese believed that Israel's view of the divine plan in history was connected to a people in a more concrete and complex fashion than was found elsewhere. In the ancient world disobedience brought automatic doom, but in Israel's history disobedience brought punishment or chastisement, but ultimately it was for the purpose of future reform not destruction.[33] In Mesopotamian materials the gods punish in order to restore a cosmic order; in Israel punishment moves people forward. John Van Seters assessed Israelite material as unique in its perception of connected events, not isolated as in some of the ancient Near Eastern sources, an overall view of history, which used the past to interpret the present (only the Babylonian Chronicle was comparable).[34] Carl Evans noted that while the west sensed the uniqueness of past events, Mesopotamiams saw them as "exemplificative," they were paradigms for the present.[35] One might conclude that Israel is bridge here, for Israel perceived events to be unique but capable of providing theological and moral exemplification.

A few words of clarification are necessary. If the point of comparison between Israel and the ancient world is reduced to the observation that Israel had historical vision which overviewed great periods of time, while the ancient Near Easterners did not, we are in error. For the Mesopotamians had chronicles which reviewed periods of history longer in duration than Israel's existence as a nation. If the comparison seeks to emphasize that Israel had a unified set of values or themes in its grand historical vision, while contemporary materials lacked this, we make a bad generalization. For the Mesopotamian chronicles can be said to have unified themes, the preservation of the cultic shrines of the deities and the maintenance of due respect. If Israel was different, it was because their historiography had more than just a "long-term policy." The suggestions of J. Roy Porter and John Hayes appear to be more precise: Israel was conscious of being an entity which underwent some development. Created within historical memory outside the land of their residence and forced to undergo many social and historic changes, the Israelites had to perceive either consciously or unconsciously that they were part of a process, which those of faith believed to be the directive presence of Yahweh. Hence, Israel has taken over the grand schemes of history provided by the ancient Near East and developed a new nuance, their God works changes in history and society and therefore must be leading them toward a goal.

5. View of God

Though it must be admitted that Israel's view of God was quite similar to the ancient Near East in most respects, nevertheless some discussions have sought to emphasize a certain facet of that perception. Henning Reventlow spoke of how Israel's view of God began to change slowly over the centuries, and this was the source of a new worldview.[36] This development, of course, was the rise of monotheism among the Israelites, a notion spearheaded by the pre-exilic and exilic prophets, which finally culminated in the exile. Many scholars point immediately to monotheism as the distinguishing characteristic of Israelite belief.[37] Frederick Moriarity asserted that the monotheistic framework allowed Yahweh to be free from the world and the forces of nature.[38] Many other authors have highlighted monotheism as the starting point for discussing many of the theological motifs believed to be unique to Israel.

110

As a concept, however, monotheism is quite broad and could include a wide matrix of ideas, many of which were discussed previously. Thus we need to delineate what particular results flow from a monotheistic faith, less we slide into easy generalizations once more. Nor can it be forgotten that monotheistic or monolatrous tendencies were found in the ancient Near East on occasion and quite frequently particular people would elevate one deity to be the "high god" and virtually ignore the rest. In these instances the characteristics of other gods would be subsumed under the nature of this one deity. So if Israel's monotheism or the process of emergent monotheism is to be used as the point of departure for discussing Israel's uniqueness, then scholars must clarify which particular concepts in the matrix of ideas are to be counted as truly significant.

Some authors have isolated particular aspects of a monotheistic faith for consideration. Patrick Miller found Israel to be unique in terms of the demand for exclusive worship of one deity with the accompanying demand for aniconic or imageless worship, both commands promulgated by the Decalogue.[39] Another way of describing the impact of monotheism is to call attention to its influence upon divination. Israel departed from the usual divinatory practices of the ancient Near East. They condemned the processes by which Yahweh might be magically manipulated. Monotheism thus brings freedom from magic.[40] Robert McFadden pointed to prophecy in Israel as the chief and unique expression of a monotheistic faith, the "major contrast between Israelite and Mesopotamian religiocultural expression."[41] But prophecy, too, could be considered as a separate category, for like monotheism it is a large institutional movement composed of many different theological understandings in a complex matrix. One of the most helpful articulations is that of Norman Gottwald, who spoke of how Yahweh became a sole high God and in this process "usurps the entire sacred domain" in order to unify people in a new social perception of reality. Though he noted the continuity of Yahweh with other high gods in the ancient world, Gottwald believed that Yahweh was portrayed as more faithful, just, and merciful, and the imagery was more oriented toward social categories rather than nature. Israel's view of God was "conceived by egalitarian sociopolitical analogies," which means the image of the deity creates equality among adherents. The image of Yahweh is of a social deity who bonds himself with people, not just kings, as elsewhere in the ancient world and the Mesopotamian chronicles. Furthermore, the will of this deity is promulgated by partisans of the egalitarian ethos, priests and prophets.[42] Gottwald has isolated the aspects of monotheism which carry social import rather than abstract ideational understandings.

Thus if we are to talk about how Israel's view of God differed, we will not simply say monotheism, but we will specify which ideas associated with monotheistic beliefs are worthy of isolation. Furthermore, it seems to this author that those of concrete social importance may be the more significant for consideration.

6. Covenant

Though scholars presently defer from speaking about covenant imagery with the enthusiasm of past generations, it still remains a possible point for discussion. A generation ago the notion of covenant was believed to have been instrumental in the formation of ideas as early as Moses, but more recently scholars have been prone to attribute most of the covenantal imagery to the Deuteronomistic Historian and other later sources. The idea of covenant in its widest sense should be understood as "election," for the concept of election by Yahweh preceded the use of the Hebrew word for covenant, *berith,* which appears to have been introduced by the prophet Hosea and the Deuteronomists.

The idea of election existed throughout the ancient Near East, kings and dynasties were elected by their patron deities; and covenants were ratified between nations with frequency. Our best examples of political covenants come from the second millennium B.C. Hittites and the first millennium B.C. Assyrians.

If we wish to speak of Israel's uniqueness in terms of covenant, as was the tendency among salvation history theologians of the past generation, we must be more nuanced. Israel inherited the idea of covenant and moved beyond contemporary societies in regard to its usage. The notion of election was expanded to include the entire people, not just kings patronized by deities, the political imagery of international covenants was theologized to describe this religious and national election of Israel.[43]

However, there are some weaknesses with this argument. If indeed, Israel did make unique contributions in the understanding of covenant, it would seem better to speak of this development as the result of some other more significant theologomena, such as their view of God, rather than making covenant the starting point for theological discussion. It appears to this author to be more of a result than a cause. Furthermore, it appears that some close analogies might be found in the ancient Near East. As discussed previously, Assyrian imperial beliefs of the first millennium B.C. portrayed Ashur as having a close bond to the Assyrian king and people with the purpose of effecting some grand manifest destiny for them. Such imagery resembles the Israelite covenantal language in no small fashion.

7. Developed Concept of the Divine Word

Significant for a few scholars would be the notion that Israel further developed the concept of the divine word of a deity. Such a view was expressed years ago by Otto Grether, who noted that although the ancient Near East had a notion of a divine word, only Israel saw that word as a force in history.[44] Only in Israel where one God was theoretically worshipped could the divine word be radically hypostatized and become the agent of divine will and purpose. Wilfrid Lambert, for example, believed that such development was found in Israel, while the rest of the ancient world never really concretized the notion. Mesopotamians still had numerous expressions for the divine word (*amatu* = word, *pu* = mouth, *qibitu* = command, and *zikru* = order) which were used in texts describing divine activity.[45] In Israel the notion of *dabar* rose to significant prominence, especially with the prophetic movement. Frederick Moriarity maintained that although Israel and the ancient Near East had the idea of a divine word efficacious in both nature and history, the content and not the medium were the point of departure for Israel's unique contribution.[46]

The observations of these scholars are accurate and interesting. But it seems that Israel's hypostatization of the divine word may have been part of a process begun in the ancient world, which would continue for years to come in those other cultures. The personification of *ma'at* in Egypt would constitute a somewhat analogous parallel to Israel's later personification of the divine word, and indicate that parallel intellectual development was occurring. Israel's use of the divine word as an agent for divine purpose may be advanced over that of her contemporaries, but what we have is a degree of difference not a unique starting point for discussion. Finally, this concept may be the result of their view of God, this theologomena may be a result not a cause.

8. Higher Piety or Morality

A totally different approach might stress the increased ethical or moral level found in the Israelite material. While the ancient Near East portrayed deities as punishing kings and nations for their neglect of cultic activity, the deity of Israel was motivated by deeper ethical norms, and a grand set of Mosaic legal traditions provided the clue to proper human behavior. (However, notice that one of the key criterion in the Deuteronomistic History is the centrality of the Jerusalem Temple in Israel's worship life and the failure of northern kings to recognize this and thus prevent their downfall.)

Several scholars have articulated opinions along this line. In his analysis of Hittite historiography Herbert Butterfield sensed a sincere piety of high moral calibre, a profound ethical sense, recognition of human finitude even among kings, but he still believed the material was inferior to comparable Israelite texts.[47] James Moyer compared Hittite and Israelite rituals and discovered similarities and differences, but he concluded in some intangible way: "Israel's religious practice is significantly different from that of her neighbors."[48]

This form of comparative analysis is extremely subjective. Our tendency to declare particular Israelite customs as morally superior results from our religious descent from those very values. We are also tempted to become myopic in our evaluation and ignore those aspects in the Hebrew Bible where a primitive morality appears to surface. As noted above, Israel's historiography also had cultic agenda as a moral criterion by which kings were assessed; it would be unfair to highlight the ethical imperatives in Deuteronomy and ignore the cultic in our comparisons. If Israelite morality is indeed superior to that of the surrounding world, and our comparison should be with Babylonian and Egyptian values rather than the degenerate customs sometimes perpetrated by neighboring Canaanites. Then it would be a matter of degree rather than substance. For it is quite evident that Israelites commonly engaged in practices found typically throughout the ancient world and received scathing derision from the prophets for their behavior. Such activity may have been the moral norm for most Israelites. Comparing morality can be very subjective.

9. Pathos

A nation which saw its formation in the gathering together of escaped slaves would naturally have a peculiar view of reality. They would be more open to the dynamic of change, since they would resent established institutions of oppression found in the ancient Near East. They would have sympathy for the oppressed. From this vantage point Walter Brueggemann presented a very creative suggestion. The new theme in

Israel's theology is the emphasis on the ability to "embrace pain," a theme in opposition to the "common theology" which legitimates social and religious structures.[49]

This analysis is certainly moving in the right direction in terms of isolating features not consonant with what we perceive as the common ancient Near Eastern theology. To refer to Israel's unique perspective as "pathos" is rather poetic; this author might choose to describe the category differently. This pathos may be part of a larger matrix of perceptions—the awareness of social and religious transformation and the openness to change in the future.

10. High Literary Quality

Some scholars emphasize a non-theological factor, the development of a new form of literature. J. Roy Porter believed that Israel was unique because this society was the first to integrate separate literary forms as found in the ancient Near East into a unified narrative. The ancient world had "raw materials" of historiography, but Israel molded them into a finished product. This narrative reflected the "real life" of "ordinary people," hence, it contained a true ethos. Only the later Islamic materials are comparable in terms of the development of such an ethos.[50] Likewise, Bertil Albrektson saw Israel to be unique in terms of the literary quality of biblical narrative. Israel imbibed of the general ancient Near Eastern notion of divine causality and omnipotence, but "what is new is rather the brilliant way of expressing this belief in historical works of a first rate literary quality."[51]

To speak of literary quality as a significant contribution is to work with a secondary product, the written results of intellectual ferment. True, Israel's historiography may be of a higher literary quality, but that would be the result of some other factors. Porter's suggestions are most helpful, because he speaks of an ethos embodied in the literature, and this is a reference to some vibrant intellectual force operative in the creation of the text. Albrektson's observations are the weak-

116

est; his conclusion would be tacitly accepted by most every-one.

D. Conclusion

From this discussion and the various observations cited the future direction of the debate may be surmised. A consensus of one or more of these perspectives may arise in future years as the mode of discussing Israel's unique perspectives. Or perhaps no consensus may arise!

Many of the positions described here could evoke further critical response from defenders of the ancient Near East and its thought. For if a notion were once articulated as a way of describing Israel's uniqueness, further evidence might be forwarded from other ancient sources to indicate a comparable insight among Israel's contemporaries. Thus careful discernment and nuanced discussion should be undertaken in this endeavor. Above all it is important that future discussion reflect the sensitive awareness of Israel's great continuity with the ancient Near Eastern world.[52]

In our discussion this author found value in most of the observations provided by scholars. However, many of the themes appear to be dependent upon some other theologomena—they are secondary characteristics. If taken together in concert with the significant themes worthy of isolation, a balanced statement of Israel's worldview may be articulated. In the opinion of this author many of these themes really demonstrate only a degree of difference between Israel and the ancient Near East not divergence. This implies that our heuristic model ought to be one of gradual development rather than revolution or radical difference. Furthermore, this author tends to be more impressed with categories which speak of concrete social experiences, social process and change. But therein we have initiated another question for scholarly discussion—the causes behind Israel's intellectual odyssey: were they ideational or social?

Notes

1. R. Rendtorff, "Entstehung," *op. cit.*, p. 746, the translation was provided by Barr, *Old and New, op. cit.*, p. 90.

2. Jon Levenson, "The Temple and the World," *Journal of Religion* 64 (1984): 281.

3. Smith, "Common Theology," *op. cit.*, pp. 135–147, and "Religious Parties," *op. cit.*, pp. 15–56.

4. R. Rentdorff, "Entstehung," *op. cit.*, pp. 735–746, and "Mose," *op. cit.*, pp. 152-171; Reventlow, "Eigenart," *op. cit.*, pp. 201–208, discussed further examples, though his conclusions were different; Gösta Ahlström, *Who Were the Israelites?* (Winona Lake, Indiana: Eisenbrauns, 1986), pp. 1–118; and Janzen, "Yoke," *op. cit.*, pp. 256–268.

5. Janzen, "Yoke," *op. cit.*, p. 257.

6. Ahlström, *Israelites, op. cit.*, p. 7.

7. Barr, *Old and New, op. cit.*, p.72.

8. Roberts, "Myth Versus History," *op. cit.*, pp. 7–8, believed that biblical theologians had overlooked the fact that Mesopotamians perceived freedom in forms of human activity which could defy the divine will.

9. *Ibid.*, p. 12, and "Cultic Manipulation," *op. cit.*, p. 181, noted the only examples of such non-mythological texts are the Prayer of Tukulti-Ninurta and his hymn to Marduk wherein the king prayed for victory over the Elamites.

10. *Idem,* "Myth Versus History," *op. cit.*, p. 4.

11. Hayes, *Introduction, op. cit.*, p. 136.

12. Koch, "Tod," *op. cit.*, pp. 100–123; and Reventlow, "Eigenart," *op. cit.*, pp. 199–217. Cf. Jacobsen, "Mesopotamian Religion," *op. cit.*, pp. 483–484.

13. Albrektson, *History, op. cit.*, pp. 115–117, but he quickly added that by placing the great saving acts in the timeless cultic context, they tended to be diluted as truly historical events.

14. Ahlström, *Israelites, op. cit.*, p. 97.

15. Moriarity, "Word," *op. cit.*, p. 359.

16. Wright, *Old Testament, op. cit.*, p. 22, and *God Who Acts, op. cit.*, pp. 48–49, actually anticipated Roberts' criticism that he failed to consider the later expressions of Babylonian religion; Wright still perceived the earlier worldview to be foundational even with the developments by the first millennium B.C.

17. Fohrer, *History, op. cit.*, p. 79.

18. Lambert, "Review," *op. cit.*, pp. 171–172.

19. Saggs, *Encounter, op. cit.*, p. 92.

20. Butterfield, *History, op. cit.*, pp. 159.

21. *Ibid.*, p. 116.

22. *Ibid.*, p. 86.

23. Drews, "Sargon," *op. cit.*, p. 387.

24. Hanson, "Apocalyptic," *op. cit.*, pp. 31–58, see especially his chart on p. 58.

25. Barr, "Revelation," *op. cit.*, p. 201.

26. Lambert, "Review," *op. cit.*, pp. 173–175.

27. Albrektson, *History, op. cit.*, pp. 77–81.

28. Butterfield, *History, op. cit.*, pp. 89, 98, 159.

29. Lindblom, *Prophecy, op. cit.*, p. 325.

30. Licht, "Biblical Historicism," *op. cit.*, pp. 109–111.

31. Porter, "Historiography," *op. cit.*, p. 131.

32. Hayes, *Introduction, op. cit.*, p. 136.

33. Gese, "Idea," *op. cit.*, pp. 62–64.

34. Van Seters, *History, op. cit.*, pp. 359–361.

35. Evans, "Naram-Sin," *op. cit.*, p. 110.

36. Reventlow, "Eigenart," *op. cit.*, pp. 199–217.

37. Porter, "Arabic," *op. cit.*, p. 21.

38. Moriarity, "Word," *op. cit.*, pp. 359–361.

39. Miller, "Israelite Religion," *op. cit.*, p. 212.

40. Uffenheimer, "Myth," *op. cit.*, pp. 156–162.

41. McFadden, "Micah," *op. cit.*, p. 133.

42. Gottwald, "Theological Task," *op. cit.*, pp. 193–194.

43. Gese, "Idea," *op. cit.*, p. 61.

44. Otto Grether, "Name und Wort Gottes im Alten Testament," Beihefte zur Zeitschrift für die alttestamentliche Wissenschaft (1934), pp. 127, 139, quoted in Moriarity, "Word," *op. cit.*, p. 354.

45. Lambert, "Review," *op. cit.*, p. 172.

46. Moriarity, "Word," *op. cit.*, pp. 359–361.

47. Butterfield, *History, op. cit.*, pp. 64, 68–69.

48. James Moyer, "Hittite and Israelite Cultic Practices: A Selected Comparison," *Scripture in Context II, op. cit.*, pp. 19-38.

49. Brueggemann, "Shape," *op. cit.*, pp. 28–46.

50. Porter, "Arabic," *op. cit.*, p. 21, and "Historiography," *op. cit.*, pp. 126–131.

51. Albrektson, *History, op. cit.*, p. 110.

52. Gottwald, "Two Models for the Origins of Ancient Israel:

Social Revolution or Frontier Development," *The Quest for the Kingdom of God: Studies in Honor of George E. Mendenhall,* eds. Herbert Huffmon, Frank Spina, and Alberto Green (Winona Lake, Indiana: Eisenbrauns, 1983), p. 7.

Chapter 9

Impetus for Change

A significant issue related to the question of how to perceive Israel's notion of salvation history and the uniqueness of concomitant theological concepts is the discussion of "why" Israel's views on divine action in history might appear to diverge from contemporary ancient Near Eastern beliefs. What was it in Israel's experience as a people that caused their peculiar religious and social value system to arise? Understanding the underlying causes for change might provide greater insight into the nature of how Israelite beliefs can be said to be different.

Scholars move in two different directions in understanding the causes behind the development of Israel's worldview. Some would explain the process in ideational or religious categories, attributing the process or break-through to a faith experience in the Exodus or a later religious intepretation of the Exodus experience. Often such scholars will speak of perceiving the source of Israel's uniqueness as an act of faith on the part of the modern reader. To say that God was active in Israel's experience to set them apart from neighboring cultures is certainly a statement of faith by a modern observer. Though many do not directly affirm this thesis, one senses that some writers, like George Ernest Wright, seek to imply that Israel was unique because of the presence of the one true God in their experience. Such an attitude fosters not only the implied moral imperative to keep the unique heritage of Israel alive today, it also encourages the scholar to contrast Israel with the surrounding environment. If God has acted decisively in Israel's history, then Israel must be decisively different.

Other scholars seek to discover a more concrete and empirical explanation for the unique matrix of ideas derived from Israel's experience. Social historians look for more scientific factors in social, political, economic, or geographic terms. Their answers appear to be more secular since they do not necessarily require a "god hypothesis" in their theorizations. Not all, however, would deny the presence of God in the experience of Israel, they merely seek those physical causes by which God might be said to have worked through the experience of ancient Israel. Such scholars are simply not satisfied with what they call an "idealistic" or non-social scientific explanation of things which have happened in a human society.

Debate may sometimes arise between these two methodological approaches even if proponents agree on a number of specific issues. For example, among advocates of the social revolutionary theory of the Israelite conquest there exists an ideological rift between George Mendenhall and Norman Gottwald. The former postulates that the religious value system of Israel was the primary catalyst in the revolutionary elan of the conquest process, while the latter sees religion and the understanding of God as merely another system derived from and expressive of the social historical experiences of people, in this case, a proletarian class struggle in ancient Palestine. Mendenhall believes that the initiative for human development runs from "religion to social reality," whereas Gottwald implies the opposite flow describes the true course of development, for religion is intrinsically a "social reality."[1] Mendenhall defends ideational causes for the origin of Israel's identity and refers to Gottwald's social-scientific reconstruction as "Procrustes' Bed of nineteenth century Marxist sociology." He considers the social-scientific approach a new religion instead of a social science.[2] The response to Mendenhall has accused him of obscuring social development with an "exclusive emphasis upon religious ideology," which has overlooked other factors due to its moralistic perspective.[3] On occasion the debate may appear to be between a believing and a nonbelieving interpretation of Israel's experience. However, it is more subtle and complex than this; many social historians wish not to speak of divine activity in a way which is not grounded in human experience, lest our discussion become mystical or appear to be an attempt to prove the existence of God for apologetic reasons. Often such social historians may have an understanding of the divine self-disclosure which perfers to see it immanent in the process (i.e., theologians who advocate history itself as revelation), so that meaningful theological talk is actually social-historical and political discussion.

For our purposes it would be helpful to briefly review some of the heuristic models proposed by scholars to account for the social and religious change in Israel. We cannot dwell upon these models in depth, for that would require a separate study in itself. Our focus shall be to discern what might be the underlying causes for the creation of a specific Israelite worldview and whether it can be said that this value system more or less developed in continuity with those cultural values of contemporary cultures.

A. Ideational Categories

Discussions which highlight an ideational component as the central catalyst in the development of Israel's worldview often speak of the notion of covenant, election, or radical monotheism. Such theologomena will be used at the starting point in a discussion of Israelite theology or the intellectual contributions imparted to suceeding generations.

Most well known is the evaluation of Walther Eichrodt. He used the notion of covenant as the over-arching paradigm into which the various ideational components of Israelite belief might be located. He saw the functionaries of the Yahweh cult as covenant mediators, and the concept of covenant was the primary category by which people defined their relationship to God.[4] Many scholars have used this model or built upon it since Eichrodt first articulated it in the 1930's.

A variation upon this theme uses the notion of election as the central focus. Less well defined than the concept of covenant, scholars sometimes feel that this notion gave rise to the later concrete expression of covenant. Israel's primary experience of being chosen by God in the beginning of the people's existence was the motivating force behind the development of later ideational and social values. Though the ancient Near East saw kings and dynasties as having a special commission or election from the divine realm, Israel expanded this to the whole people. Election, like covenant, emphasizes the special relationship of a people to the deity and demands that they exhibit their new and separate identity. Certainly the cultic prescriptions of Leviticus and the social legislation of Deuteronomy declare this to be the case. Salvation history theologians in the past generation used the language of covenant to a great extent when speaking of Israel's uniqueness. If proposed today, the notion would not be used to catalog a host of differences between Israel and the ancient Near East, but it would be seen as they key ingredient which caused Israelite thought to develop in the direction it did. Even a critic like John Van Seters pointed to this as a peculiar characteristic of Israelite thought.[5]

Another avenue of approach in describing the central focus in Israel's value system is to isolate monotheism as the ideological inspiration for Israelite identity. The classic work is that of William Foxwell Albright, who envisioned the "monotheistic revolution" brought about by Moses as the beginning of the entire Israelite intellectual tradition. He saw this as a radical break or great leap forward in the pre-monarchical period, which would subsequently affect the entire ethos. The monotheistic faith advocated in the Mosaic period would be just as developed as that found at the time of the rabbis.[6] In similar fashion Yehezkal Kaufmann analyzed the history of Israelite religion from the perspective of a pure and radical monotheism which he believed permeated the bulk of Israelite society from the conquest forward. Any signs of apparent idolatry or syncreticism in the pre-exilic period were only superstitious fetishism, not true idolatry, for so firmly had monotheism been planted in the minds of the people.[7] Recently Irving Zeitlin has followed the direction of Kaufmann in his assessment of Israelite beliefs, which contrasts Israel quite strongly to the religious beliefs of surrounding ancient Near Eastern cultures.[8] (The Kaufmann School of thought has had few followers in this rather extremely stated position.) Monotheism is indeed a significant aspect of Israelite thought which separated them from the surrounding environment. But if monotheism arose slowly among the bulk of the Israelite population, as scholars now perceive, then it cannot be said to have been the precipitating factor in the development of the Israelite ethos, but rather it was the result of a different process.

Ideational categories may be helpful in making general theological summations of the Israelite value system, but one has the sense that they are the resultant product. Notions like covenant and monotheism appear to have arisen late in the pre-exilic period or the exile. Hence, perhaps some other facet of thought or some concrete social process might be evaluated as the precipitating agent in the formation of Israelite values.

B. Social-Historical Categories

Concrete explanations for the development of Israel and the concomitant value system are provided by scholars more attuned to the social sciences. Such scholars would see the historical and social experiences of people in human situations give rise to the thought which best summarized and gave meaning to their experience.

An early assessment in this regard was given by the famous sociologist Max Weber in his *Ancient Judaism*. He implied that since Israel was not an old river-valley culture, it was not burdened with fixed social and economic structures of a highly organized and bureaucratic state. Egypt and Mesopotamia needed authoritarian structures to sustain sophisticated irrigation systems necessary for agricultural production and survival. Israel was a "peripheral" highland culture which survived without these burdensome structures, so they could permit greater freedom for individuals and groups within the society, and subsequently develop an ethos which would encourage social growth and radical social and economic equality. As a "peripheral culture" they had access to the great intellectual and technological contributions of their ancient Near Eastern neighbors, and they could put them together in a fresh fashion.[9] Subsequent analysis of the ancient Near East, and in part, Israel, by economic historians has tended to reinforce the model proposed by Weber.[10]

Social historians have often described later ancient Near Eastern history as an "axial age," the era in which great ideas were created and the modern world was born. The great social and intellectual breakthrough, according to some, occurred in this axial age under certain circumstances. Axial age civilizations have semi-nomadic or pastoralist origins, live in proximity to a high culture, experience quick social change in their settlement process, have a core of intellectual leaders generating a new or renewed ethos, and are stimulated by contact with an imperial state.[11] Such a description fits Israel aptly—they settled in Palestine (or arose out of the indigenous people), existed between Mesopotamian and Egyptian cultural spheres, quickly acculturated to Canaanite customs which evoked a nostalgic Yahwistic movement, and prophets, priests, and levites generated political and theological beliefs which were fertilized and galvanized by the expansion of the Assyrian and Persian empires with their imperialistic value systems. The intellectual heritage of the ancient world is apprehended and rearticulated in this process.

The grand scheme can be refined even further with the aid of sociological theory. The macro-sociologist Gerhard Lenski described how the use of iron and the invention of the iron plow especially creates an "advanced agrarian society" wherein stratified society evolves.[12] Israel experienced this cultural development but retained an old pastoralist egalitarian

126

value system. Lenski noted that "herding societies' (pastoralists) tend not only to have a greater degree of equality, but they often are monotheistic.[13] In his system herding societies are not in the mainstream of social development but remain an offshoot, a reaction against early or advanced agrarian society. This merger of Israel, a "herding society,' into the social system of an "advanced agrarian society" created the tension and ideological conflict which gave birth to the Yahwistic movement and its theology.

Biblical scholars have used these and similar categories to assess the development of the Israelite state and society. Frank Crüsemann evaluated early Israel as a "segmentary society," a category comparable to Lenski's early agrarian model, which existed prior to the rise of the Israelite state.[14] In even more nuanced fashion Frank Frick traced the pre-monarchic Israelite society through the stages of "segmentary society" and "chiefdom" before evolving into a state.[15] Other scholars likewise have used sociological perspectives in their evaluation of Israel.[16]

Herbert Butterfield described the rise of Israelite historiography in similar fashion before the current fascination with sociological models. He noted that the people Israel came into the ancient Near Eastern scene quite late and inherited what developed in the previous years. But since they led a simple sedentary life after settlement, they did not "go through the intermediate stages that made progress so slow in other countries."[17] In their historiography Israel progressed farther than the royal annalists of the Hittites and Assyrians. Thus again one may speak of Israel's ability to inherit and modify what preceded in the religious and intellectual environment.

Some scholars use this social historical approach and speak even more directly in social, political, and economic categories. Some recent biblical scholars advocate the use of the social scientific method as the necessary avenue of approach in the study of Israel's literature and belief.[18] Norman Gottwald, in particular, used the social scientific method and opposed "idealism," the treatment of the religion of Yahweh as a thing unto itself without consideration of the social categories. He declared boldly that biblical criticism without sociological criticism was circular exegesis and merely empty theology, lacking true historical evaluation to undergird it.[19] It has been said that if Julius Wellhausen broke with "naive precritical historicism" and William Albright broke with "evolutionism," then Norman Gottwald may be said to have broken with "idealism" in his move toward "religious functionalism."[20] In a similar vein Frank Frick asserted that:

> . . . religious thought has suffered greatly by having been rather unceremoniously ripped out of any systematic setting, with little or no attempt to formulate general relationships between religious actions and social processes.[21]

The social scientific approach has thus produced many fine assessments of the Israelite state, their social values, and the evolution of thought.[22] This approach may be the direction of future biblical research in this area.

Concerning the question of analyzing Israel's intellectual relationship to the ancient world a number of scholars before Gottwald had used social-historical categories as their primary approach. Nicolas Wyatt and Manfred Weippert perceived that Israel may have differed from the ancient Near East in terms of social distinctions. When Israelite theologians had reflected upon the experience of both the conquest of the land and the later exile, these social values were the dominant factors which affected and helped created Israel's views and the different form of historiography.[23] Of course, such would not be obvious to us in reading the text, since those ancient theologians did not use the social-historical language we would recognize. But there was an awareness that God had created a new society wherein the relationship of people to Yahweh and to each other was different from anything which preceded it. Israel had the same intellectual traditions and the old model for preparing court annals (historiography) as did other West-Semitic people, but their crystalizing experience came with the exile, and other nations did not have such a comparable

128

motivation to create a grand literary historiography which embodied the ethos of a people.[24]

Norman Gottwald's thorough social-scientific approach of Israel's origins, epitomized in his work *The Tribes of Yahweh,* represent this methodology in its classic form. He viewed Israel's new identity to be a result of a class-struggle between Yahwistic pastoralists and disenfranchised El-worshipping Canaanites (or *Hapiru*) on the one hand and statist, class-oriented, mercantilistic, Canaanite oppressors on the other. His Marxist based critique saw the creation of Israel and its unique religious values as the result of a classic proletarian revolution.[25] Such an evaluation surely reduces Israel's unique worldview to an experience available to the tools and theoretic models of social-scientific research.

The work of social historians provides us with concrete heuristic models by which to understand the rise of the Israelite value system. But we still have a range of options from which to choose. Some scholars use the social historical model in a limited way to understand certain important dynamics operative in the creation of the Israelite people. Others use the social-scientific categories in a very rigorous fashion, and in so doing, they must use particular theoretical models and apply them stringently. The danger of the first approach is to use social models in a generalized and haphazard fashion, so as to produce explanations built upon evidence taken slightly out of context. The danger of the second approach is to possibly straightjacket the biblical materials into a theoretical model which may not really fit their social cultural experience. The critique often levelled against Gottwald's approach is that he makes the Israelites sound very much like modern peasant revolutionaries rather than people of the early Iron Age. Despite these reservations the social historical approach offers great potential for future research and understanding the rise of the Israelite ethos.

C. Conclusion

The debate between the ideational and the social-historical approachs to understanding the origin of the Israelite identity

may never be resolved, and the distinction may actually pro-
mote a false dichotomy. When speaking of the mechanism by
which Israel set forth with a new ethos, one ought to combine
both ideational and social-historical categories in the discussion. For it may well be necessary to use both when discussing
the complex experience of human beings. Whether ideational
forces gave rise to social-historical realities or the reverse
remains an unanswerable question.

Ideational and concrete social factors arise together and
cross-fertilize each other. Furthermore, it is more realistic to
admit that when dealing with vast movements of people over
several centuries different segments of society are primarily
influenced and motivated by religious beliefs while others are
moved by social forces. The scholar who works with these
models is trying to use abstract heuristic paradigms to cover
the infinitely complex human process.

If forced to make a distinction for pedagogical reasons,
however, this author would prefer to speak of the social
historical factors first and then the ideational categories. This
is not to imply that ideational categories are any less important. Rather it is to admit that the intellectual concepts which
inspire people and provide them with their self-identity do not
arise in a vacuum, but they result from a process of development fueled by the concrete historical experiences of a people.
Notions like covenant, election, and monotheism are para-
mount, and they do sum up the belief system of ancient Israel
better than anything else. But they arose as grand notions to
encapsulate and epitomize the experience of the struggling
people Israel. They may represent the result of a faith struggle
of an entire people, but individuals within that group moved
toward the intellectual goal often for very simple and concrete
reasons.

Notes

1. Brueggemann, "Theological Issues in The Tribes of Yahweh by
N. K. Gottwald: Four Critical Responses," *The Bible and Liberation,*

op. cit., pp. 176–177; and Anderson, "Mendenhall Disavows Paternity: Says He Didn't Father Gottwald's Marxist Theory," *Bible Review* 2, #2 (Summer, 1986); 46–49.

2. Mendenhall, "Migration Theories vs. Culture Change as an Explanation for Early Israel," *Society of Biblical Literature 1976 Seminar Papers,* ed. George MacRae (Missoula, Montana: Scholars Press, 1976), pp. 135–143, and "Ancient Israel's Hyphenated History," *Palestine in Transition: The Emergence of Ancient Israel,* The Social World of Biblical Antiquity Series, vol. 2 (Sheffield, England: Almond, 1983), pp. 91 et 91–103.

3. Marvin Chaney, "Ancient Palestinian Peasant Movements and the Formation of Premonarchic Israel," *Palestine in Transition, op. cit.,* pp. 49–51.

4. Eichrodt, *Theology of the Old Testament,* 2 vols., trans. James Baker (Philadelphia: Westminster, 1961–1967), 1:25–520, 2:15–529.

5. Van Seters, *History, op. cit.,* pp. 360–361.

6. Albright, *Stone Age, op. cit.,* pp. 1–403.

7. Yehezkal Kaufmann, *The Religion of Israel: From its Beginning to the Babylonian Exile,* trans. and abr. Moshe Greenberg (New York: Schocken, 1972), pp. 7–149.

8. Zeitlin, *Judaism, op. cit.,* pp. 1–106.

9. Max Weber, *Ancient Judaism,* trans. and ed. Hans Gerth and Don Martindale (Glencoe, Illinois: Free Press, 1952), pp. xvii–xix, 7–8, 252–263; and Gnuse, *You Shall Not Steal: Community and Property in the Biblical Tradition* (Maryknoll, New York: Orbis, 1985), pp. 53–58, built upon these same presuppositions in this evaluation.

10. Karl Wittfogel, *Oriental Despotism* (New Haven: Yale, 1957), pp. 1–449, would concur with Weber, for he analyzed ancient Near Eastern societies as "hydraulic economies," where authoritarian government developed to maintain control over water resources; William Davisson and James Harper, *European Economic History,* vol. 1: *The Ancient World* (New York: Appleton-Century-Crofts, 1972), pp. 30–85, described ancient Near Eastern economic systems as "status-redistributive" or "storehouse" economies, and pointed out that Israel was the first to deviate from this pattern; and T. F. Carney, *The Economics of Antiquity: Controls, Gifts, and Trade* (Lawrence, Kansas: Coronado, 1973), pp. 20–21, described the ancient Near Eastern economic system quite well as a redistributive economy based on class structures.

11. Hermann Kulke, "The Historical Background of India's Axial Age," *Axial Age, op. cit.,* pp. 390–391.

12. Gerhard and Jean Lenski, *Human Societies: An Introduction to Macrosociology*, 3rd ed. (New York: McGraw-Hill, 1978), pp. 189–230; but David Hopkins, *The Highlands of Canaan: Agricultural Life in the Early Iron Age*, The Social World of Biblical Antiquity Series, vol. 3 (Sheffield, England: Almond, 1985), pp. 15–275, warned us not to rely too heavily upon specific technological advances as answers to why Israel developed in the highlands of Canaan, rather these breakthroughs must be seen as operating in concert with a newly developing social organization, the tribal structures of early Israel.

13. Lenski and Lenski, *Human Societies, op. cit.*, pp. 237–238.

14. Frank Crüsemann, *Der widerstand gegen das Königtum: Die antiköniglichen Texte des Alten Testamentes und der Kampf um der frühen israelitischen Staat*, Wissenschaftliche Monographien zum Alten und Neuen Testament, vol. 49 (Neukirchen Vluyn: Neukirchener, 1978), pp. 201–215.

15. Frank Frick, *The Formation of the State in Ancient Israel: A Survey of Models and Theories*, The Social World of Biblical Antiquity Series, vol. 4 (Sheffield, England: Almond, 1985), pp. 51–204.

16. Ahlström, *Israelites, op. cit.*, pp. 1–118; and Chaney, "Peasant Movements," *op. cit.*, pp. 39–90.

17. Butterfield, History, *op. cit.*, p. 90. Hayes *Introduction, op. cit.*, p. 36, also noted that the late arrival of Israel in the arena of ancient Near Eastern culture provides an explanation for their relative advance over other cultures.

18. Chaney, "Systemic Study of the Israelite Monarchy," *Semeia* 37 (1986): 54–57; and Gottwald, "The Participation of Free Agrarians in the Introduction of Monarchy to Ancient Israel: An Application of H. A. Landsberger's Framework for the Analysis of Peasant Movements," *Semeia* 37 (1986): 77–106.

19. Gottwald, "Social Matrix and Canonical Shape," *Theology Today* 42 (1985): 307–321.

20. Brueggemann, "Theological Issues," *op. cit.*, pp. 173–174.

21. Frick, *Formation, op. cit.*, p. 14.

22. Gottwald, "Early Israel and 'The Asiatic Mode of Production' in Canaan," *Society of Biblical Literture 1976 Seminar Papers, op. cit.*, pp. 145–154, and "Early Israel and the Canaanite Socio-economic System," *Palestine in Transition, op. cit.*, pp.25–37; Chaney, "Peasant Movements," *op. cit.*, pp. 39–90, and "Monarchy," *op. cit.*, pp. 53–76; Frick, *Formation, op. cit.*, pp.13–204; and Ahlström, *Israelites, op. cit.*, pp. 1–118.

23. Manfred Weippert, "Fragen des israelitischen Geschichtsbewusstseins," *Vetus Testamentum* 23 (1973): 415–442; and Wyatt, "Observations," *op. cit.,* p. 832.

24. Wyatt, "Observations," *op. cit.,* p. 832.

25. Gottwald, *The Tribes of Yahweh: A Sociology of Liberated Israel, 1250–1050 B.C.E.* (Maryknoll, New York: Orbis, 1979), pp. 3–916, and "Free Agrarians," *op. cit.,* pp. 77–106.

Chapter 10
General Conclusions

Thus far we have traced a debate from the eager affirmation of salvation history models by biblical theologians, through the critique of those who would defend the integrity of ancient Near Eastern thought, to the point where biblical theologians must now speak with greater sensitivity and precision of Israel's view of salvation history in relation to the ancient Near Eastern setting. Attendant upon this view of salvation history are many other notions, including perspectives on cult, sacrifice, morality, law, human equality, and social relations. Here, too, scholars in the past generation had been wont to stress Israel's distinctiveness, but now greater continuity has been recognized. Scholars can no longer speak of Israel's uniqueness on a broad spectrum of issues connected to the salvation history paradigm. Rather a more nuanced approach must carefully select those points of divergence and more precisely define how Israel's understanding moves beyond the ancient world in regard to those issues. Only in this way will the greater umbrella of salvation history theology be presented in objective and judicious fashion. At this present time there still appears to be diversity of opinion; some scholars use the old dichotomies, others speak of great continuity. What direction should be taken from this point?

In this chapter a few tentative general observations will be presented as guidelines for future discussion. This author is tempted to adopt a moderate position in the debate. While admitting the great continuity of Israel's thought with the ancient world, somehow the notion of general human development coupled with an awareness of the Israelite intellectual heritage implies that Israel took a qualitative step forward in terms of religious and intellectual evolution. When one compares the basic practices most commonly found in the ancient Near East with those values endorsed by at least the prophetic minority in Israel, one is impressed by the divergence, even if it is not as complete as we had been wont to say in the past. How to articulate this by clearly and sensitively describing that transformation remains the difficult challenge.

A primary consideration would entail a call for moderation. Past generations may have made excessive claims concerning Israel's uniqueness and the *Heilsgeshichte* perspective, their contributions to intellectual development, such as the notion of God, history, and human identity. The contrasts between Israel and the ancient Near East may have been too stark. But we must not now move to the other extreme by denying the importance of Israel's historical or linear view of reality. The critique of most scholars critical of the salvation history paradigm in the last generation has been sober, objective, and balanced. Most have not denied the significance of Israel's contributions, rather they have called for a more accurate portrayal. Their work has laid the foundation for such a quest. Israelite thought was different, not unique; it moved beyond ancient Near Eastern values in certain respects, but it was not diametrically opposed to the values of predecessor cultures.

A. History as a Term in the Discussion

Israel's perspective was not historical as we would understand the notion, but it was linear or "proto-historical." Comparative studies mentioned throughout this work which considered the ancient Near Eastern and Greek historiographical accomplishments indicated that biblical materials moved beyond the level of Mesopotamian history-writing but fell short of the Greek historians. We have a mixed verdict on the Hittite materials; most would consider biblical materials more advanced (i.e., Herbert Butterfield), but Hittite specialists claim the Hittites to be forerunners to the Greeks and superior to the Israelites. At any rate, we have a spectrum of quality in reference to these historiographical materials. There is a progression from the earlier Mesopotamian to the later Israelite and Hittite, and finally the Greek sources can claim to be history in the truest sense. Biblical materials lie on an evolutionary continuum.

To be more precise we ought to avoid calling the biblical material "history" and reserve that term for the later Greek historians. In the past the word *Geschichte* was used to describe proto-historical materials in distinction to the word *Historie,* a term for more accurate, objective, scientific history (if such can be said to ever exist!). This would be a good distinction to use today, but for the fact that the English speaking world tends to use the terminology differently than do the Germans. In the past many biblical theologians used the term *Geschichte* to describe biblical materials, and they proceeded to discuss the biblical accounts as though they were actual, observable events rather than the popular folkloristic accounts to which the term *Geschichte* refers. Theologians were tempted to regard the narrative materials as factual historical accounts because they wished to avoid a view which permitted little or no factual event to lie behind the text. This direction was taken by Gerhard von Rad and Rudolf Bultmann on the continent, and their views alienated or frightened the more conservative scholars in the English-speaking world. So the move to a more conservative viewpoint arose in the Biblical Theology Movement, which sought a higher level of facticity in the primal salvific events. Because of the usage of the terms *Geschichte* and *Historie* in the past generation, it might be best to simply drop these terms.

Because of our desire to affirm a high degree of facticity behind the biblical accounts, we were unable to appreciate the level of development found in the biblical "historiographical" accounts. We wished to perceive them as more advanced forms of history writing than they were. Though we might have used the term *Geschichte* to describe the biblical materi-

137

als, we never let the full implications of this term manifest themselves. In the future, if we are to retain *Heilsgeschichte* paradigms, we must be ready to deal with the very critical questions of facticity raised by von Rad and Bultmann. We need to speak in a more tentative fashion about Israel's concept of history and the corresponding historiographical literature in the Bible. Both were products of an early stage of human development. Israel's history-writing was developmentally speaking quite prior to historiography as we would recognize it.

If we continue to use the word *Heilsgeschichte,* we should imbue it consciously with this meaning, or we ought to choose another word to clearly delineate Israel's literature apart from "history" as we know it. A better word is linear, a term frequently used in the discussion. It carries the connotation of being different than cyclic or mythic material, but it carries fewer implications of advanced development than the term "history." Use of the term linear would imply something proto-historical, a bridge in the evolution of true history-writing.

B. The Linear Perspective

Israel did not invent this linear perspective but adopted it from the surrounding intellectual milieu. Certainly the evidence offered by ancient Near Eastern historians indicates that the Hittites and Assyrians especially saw the gods as intervening in history and punishing people for past events. The Assyrians also seem to have had a notion of manifest destiny for their nation. Both visions imply a degree of linearity. What Israel did was give this perspective greater emphasis. Certainly the Deuteronomistic Historians provided a document which is more extensive and is permeated more thoroughly with the ideas of divine action in the scope of human events over a period of time. Israel inherited these notions and advanced them. We must not place Israel's understanding in diametric opposition to neighboring cultures in this regard!

Israel's early monolatry and the later emergent monotheism may have permitted a view of God which freed the deity from identification with the forces of nature to a greater extent than in other cultures, and this may have permitted a greater use of linear imagery. Though Yahweh was still described with nature imagery, he may have been less tightly connected to it as elsewhere in the ancient world. Thus the linear or proto-historical perspective could become a more dominant theme in Israel's thought. Thus we shall say that Israel had this perspective in a more thoroughgoing but not exclusive way.

C. Reconstruction as a Model

Israel's form of intellectual contribution might be best de-scribed as a reconstruction or reconstrual of previous thought rather than an epigenesis or breakthrough, as George Ernest Wright had described it.[2] When biblical theologians spoke of Israel as making a radical breakthrough, they were forced to search for that which was "unique" in Israel's thought, and forced generalizations were the result. We should not search for the new and the unique in Israel but perceive how old ideas were placed in a new construct, and how different ideas were brought to the fore in fresh fashion.[3]

All of Israel's significant themes may be found in the ancient Near East: divine intervention in history, divine purpose or plan for human society, the demand for social justice, a sense of human equality, and the impetus for the rise of monotheism. Those themes might have been previously expressed in the ancient Near Eastern societies as secondary or minor themes in a given ideological-social construct, but now in Israelite belief they received a greater or primary emphasis.

The notion of a reconstruction or reconstrual of thought by the ancient Israelite theologians has been voiced by other scholars as a possible heuristic model. Abraham Malamat spoke of Israel bringing historiography to a new "artistic perfection."[4] Klaus Koch described Israel as drawing her beliefs from the ancient Near East, but in this new construction the sum was greater than the original parts.[5] John Hayes noted that Israel was a latecomer to the ancient Near East, who could inherit the values and move beyond the contemporary cultures because of the historical experience of the people.[6] Frank Cross perceived that Israel emerged from the old matrix of Canaanite beliefs and adapted them in new form.[7] J. Roy Porter believed that Israel consciously developed an awareness that her creation was the result of successive stages of development and growth.[8] This even implies that the Israelites were aware of their own process of reconstruction. Norman Gottwald called for a careful nuance in the discussion of Israel's relation to the thought of the predecessor cultures, since many Canaanites and their cultural values contributed to the construction of Israel's new value system.[9] Many Israelite values may have been determined by a reaction against the ideology of the city states of Canaan and a deliberate reformulation of those values. Walter Brueggemann even used imagery comparable to this author when he spoke of Israel's "transmutation" and "mutation" of inherited values as the struggle developed to break free from the "common theology" of the ancient Near East which legitimated such structures.[10] Frank Frick's social scientific model of Israel's political evolution spoke of "adaptive modification," "adaptive transformation," and "adaptive adjustment."[11] From a broad social historical perspective Shmuel Eisenstadt described how Israel provided a significant breakthrough in the "axial age" by restructuring thought and social values taken from the ancient world.[12] Finally, Patrick Miller summarized it best:

> . . . various strands and aspects of the ancient Near Eastern world—clan religion, Hittite treaties, and Baal imagery—came together in a complex way. The particularity of Israel's religion is in the result of all this coming together, not in any single element, which can always be paralleled. . . . Israel's religious

origins and particularity must be seen in and through the religious world and not only over against it.[13]

As we use these terms of reconstruction or reconstrual, we must not forget that the process of transformation took centuries during the pre-exilic period. Some contemporary biblical scholars firmly remind us of the nature of this evolutionary or developmental advance.[14] Though we may speak of the transformation in graphic terms, we must not forget that it was a long historical process.

D. Elements of Continuity

Nor must we forget the value of some of the elements inherited in unchanged fashion by Israel. Silence in the polemics of Israelite literature on many issues implies that much of the "common theology" was absorbed. Israelite thought participated in the common thought of the ancient world in decisive ways, for here Israel obtained its basic ways of perceiving reality. "Common theology" addressed human need by providing a basis for legitimating social structures and providing moral coherence. There are simply basic universal ways of perceiving reality in rational and coherent fashion.[15] Walter Brueggemann saw a dialectic of how Israelite theology participated in this "common theology" yet struggled to be free of it: the tension was between views which legitimated social and ideational structures and those Israelite views which accepted pathos and embraced pain. Yet he warned against facile evaluations of Israel's thought by contrasting these two elements, because the process of transformation had been complex and both aspects had become truly Israelite ways of viewing reality.[16]

With this understanding of Israelite thought as a reconstruction of ancient Near Eastern beliefs, perhaps old issues might be approached in a new fashion.[17] Israel's monotheism would be discussed in relation to the ancient Near Eastern tendency to elevate a high god like Aten, Seth, Marduk, Ashur, or Ninurta, rather than emphasizing the contrast between Yahweh worship and simple polytheism.[18] Israel's historiography could be discussed as a more expanded and extensive theological interpretation of the past comparable to Egyptian, Babylonian, Assyrian, and Hittite counterparts in many respects. Israel's call for justice might be seen as an extension of ancient Near Eastern cries for reform, which Israel attempted on a larger scale in a smaller country, an attempt grander than had been tried previously. Continuity would be the hallmark of our discussion on these issues.

E. Israel As a Peripheral Society

This reconstruction was possible because Israel was a fresh, new society, relatively speaking, a "peripheral people" on the edge of great civilizations. They inherited ancient values but were not bound to the old, established social-economic-political structures and solutions to life's problems. As pastoralists entering the land or as Canaanites withdrawing from old decadent Bronze Age city states, they were in position to reconstruct a new matrix out of the old ideas.[19] Israel was not burdened by the complex social structures found in the river valley cultures of Egypt and Mesopotamia. They were free to be more innovative and implement new idealistic values. This dynamic also explains why similar advances appear among the Hittites and the Greeks.[20] All were peripheral cultures at the edge of the great, advanced, older civilizations, and they absorbed high ideas and forged them into a new matrix.

Israel arose at a critical juncture in human history; the end of the Bronze Age and the beginning of the Iron Age brought potential not only for technological and social advancement but also for ideational progress.[21] Such development occurred throughout the cultural sphere from the Mediterranean to East Asia in what modern historians have termed the "Axial Age." Israel was a newly organized group of people who had quickly and violently withdrawn from a burned out Bronze Age society. Their proximity to high cultures enabled them to absorb the old values, and their intellectual leaders (the Yahwistic minority) slowly reshaped these values into a new system under the encroachment of Assyrian and Persian imperial states. The survival of this people was made possible by the assumption of these values by the greater population during and after the exile.[22] Israel created nothing new, rather they had a "fresh beginning with old materials." The reconstruction of the best values of the old order created a vigorous new ethos.

The language of contemporary social-historical models may be used effectively in our study. Use of sociological and anthropological models enable us to see more readily the similarity and continuity between cultures, which then assists scholars to more precisely observe the nuance of difference.

There are different ways to speak of Israel as such a "peripheral" people in relation to the ancient world. Certainly their own self-definition as a nation forged from escaped slaves indicates a self-understanding designed to set them apart from typical ancient Near Eastern values. Regardless of which view of the conquest is assumed, whether it be violent conquest by invasion, peaceful infiltration, internal revolution, or peaceful withdrawal, the core of people who became Israel were a community set in opposition to the values of their local Palestinian environment to some degree, which in turn reflected the generic values of the ancient world. Some scholars emphasize the pastoral origins of the Israelites, a background which gave them an impetus toward equality, corporate solidarity, and social concern, which then placed them in opposition to the values of a sedentary society with its orientation toward a fertility emphasis in the cult, central storehouse and mercantilistic economics, and a class oriented society. Some scholars emphasize the indigenous or internal origin of Israelites in the land of Palestine as alienated Canaanites, in which case their regard for the established values of the ancient Near East would be hostile in a selective sense according to the reasons

143

for their alienation. At any rate one might perceive Israel as a peripheral people who were ready to reconstruct ancient Near Eastern values in a new matrix.

F. Retention of Primitive Elements

Israel did not discard immediately all of the old, primitive, magical elements of ancient thought. These earlier elements continued throughout much of pre-exilic Israelite development as a legitimate expression of common Israelite belief and practice. The prophetic-priestly Yahwistic tradition remained a minority movement until after the exile.[23] It would thus be better to describe Israel's arrival at this new ethos as one of gradual transformation or evolution. The best model by which to understand this process is not the older perception of evolution as a slow, inevitable, uniform movement upward as one new mutation after another is slowly added. Rather the more contemporary model of genetic evolution is preferable. Herein individual mutations occur slowly and remain as recessive or latent in the genetic pool of an animal population, until they arise together in a newly construed matrix which enables them to become dominant genetic factors. What appears as a jump in the evolutionary development is actually the result of a prior process which leads to a moment of precipitation. Thus development occurs gradually but manifests itself in what appears to quick "jumps" or "leaps" in the evolutionary process.[24]

This model has been used by social historians to describe the development of human societies. Eli Sagan has observed the following scheme of social development: primitive societies, early complex societies, later complex societies, and archaic societies.[25] This would probably correspond to Gerhard Lenski's model of hunting and gathering societies (primitive) horticultural societies (complex) and simple agrarian societies (archaic).[26] For Sagan quantum leaps occur between human stages of development which require a degree of energy not necessary for gradual evolution. Slow change may occur within these stages, but quantum leaps require much more energy—"universal bursts of energy . . . fuel the advance to the next stage."[27] Such a model could be used to describe Israel. The inheritance of old values in the previous Bronze Age environment were collected by various segments of the population; with the demise of Bronze Age cultures and urban life these new values became to come together in a new matrix which produced a quantum leap.

The genetic analogy applied to the social historical model may serve as a pedagogical tool to describe Israel's ideological journey over the period of six centuries (1200–600 B.C.). Israel inherited many ideas from the ancient Near East which were present in a recessive fashion, but the peripheral experience of Israel permitted a reconstruction of these values and allowed them to surface over the short span of a few centuries to become the new ethos of Israel. The exile provided the catalyst for the complete emergence of a new worldview. Hence, Israel may appear different from other contemporary cultures, when in reality all of the so-called "unique" ideas were really present already in the ancient Near East.

G. Heuristic Value of the Reconstructive Model

Use of this model can be seen as an attempt to accommodate various perspectives of previous scholars. Some have spoken of how Israel's development was a slow, evolutionary process.[28] This model retains those perceptions, in part. Yet it emphasizes how this reconstruction surfaces in human history with a radical sense of departure from previous values. (Realistically, to speak of a six hundred year developmental process in the scope of millions of years of human evolution is a rather "quick" development.) The full reconstruction or mutation of Israel finally arose in the exile. The model enables us to speak of the "newness" or "uniqueness" of Israelite belief by permitting us to see how Israel moved beyond the values of contemporary cultures without pejoratively portraying those societies and their beliefs.

When this evolutionary model is used one may not only regard the ancient Near East more sympathetically, but also portray their mode of contributing to the "new" ethos of Israel in a positive fashion (albeit dialectical). As ancient Near Eastern scholars have indicated, the values in the ancient world changed over the millennia. With the emergence of more complex states and the creation of writing as a mode of communication the more primitive, sympathetic magic gave way to more social and anthropomorphic views of religion, the world, and society. The ancient Near East does not present for our consideration a worldview which is purely "mythic" or "cyclic" as biblical theologians were wont to stereotype it. Already when Israel entered the scene the worldview was in transition, it had a "broken cyclic" orientation.[29] The ancient Near East provided Israel with the raw materials for their creative advance. In this way the ancient world might be viewed not in opposition to Israel but in continuity, contributing the world view which would ultimately transcend its parent culture. Israel would in turn perform the same function for western civilization.

Israel simply moved to a higher level than her contemporaries, or better said, Israel continued the creative advance. By the reconstruction of received values Israel continued the evolutionary advance with a qualitatively better perception of the world and society.

H. Conclusion

In sum we postulate that Israel did not invent a worldview in contrast to ancient Near Eastern thought but rather drew upon existing ideas and reconstructed them. They had a fresh beginning with old and traditional values which provided social and moral advancement. Dominant emphasis was given to ideas previously found subordinate in the ancient Near Eastern

146

intellectual matrix for social, political, economic, and religious reasons. Israel was essentially a new society not bounded by established standards and structures of societies millennia old, hence a reconstruction was possible. The parallel with Greece might be drawn, for here was another society on the cultural periphery.

Thus we are advocating that Israel was part of a spectrum, where one might observe "gradual" but "significant" advances on the path of long and arduous development. This is not simple evolution, but more comparable to the macroevolution described by some geneticists.

With this approach we might discuss the notion of salvation history in a more precise and sensitive fashion and thus synthesize the critique of ancient Near Eastern scholars with the attempt of biblical theologians to apprehend our roots.

I. Postscript

This discussion provides extremely significant input for other issues of study in biblical theology. One might especially think of a consideration of the development of monotheism. First, Israel's monotheism is not something to be compared drastically in opposition to the polytheism of the ancient Near East, as has often been done in the past. Rather one should perceive the impetus toward monolatry or even monotheism in the ancient world long before Israel's existence. Instances would include: 1) the cult of Ptah in Heracleopolis in Egypt around 2800 B.C., 2) the cult of Marduk in Babylon during the Amorite and Kassite periods of the second millennium B.C., 3) the so-called Amarna revolution of Akhnaton which elevated the sun disk Aten above the other deities in Egypt during the fourteenth century B.C. (so-called because it appears this revolution may have been the culmination of a very long established intellectual tradition), 4) the elevation of the deity Seth in the twelfth century B.C. Ramsesside Egypt, 5) the cults of Ashur and Ninurta in Assyria, and in other instances

147

where a particular group emphasized a "universal high god," who absorbed, reflected, epitomized, or actually dominated the divinity of rival gods in the same pantheon without necessarily rejecting the existence of those deities.

Second, the development of monotheism in Israel was a gradual and uneven process not accomplished in one great moment. To perceive monotheism arising full-blown with Moses or some other figure is as naive as simple evolutionary schemes which postulate a gradual movement through various levels ascending toward pure monotheism. This new model would admit that for much of Israel's pre-exilic experience polytheism, henotheism, or the concept of a national high god was the normative belief for the majority of Israelites and not just an aberration, superstition, or backsliding. Monolatry or monotheism was the possession of a small group or cadre of Yahweh devotees who sought to expand their exclusivistic tendenz to wider circles. They created the literature which would imply that this monotheism was the possession of believers from the Mosaic period onward. Even among this group were not to be found pure monotheists at all times, for the creative advance was very uneven. The spread of monotheism to the greater society was accomplished gradually over the years and abetted by signal events and crises in the history of the people, such as the conquest, the incursion of Phoenician Baalism in the ninth century B.C., the prophetic movement, Deuteronomic reform, and the exile. Monotheism became established among the general populace as the theological norm only with the exile and post-exilic periods.

Such a study would become a good case example of the general observations made by this work. It could demonstrate how Israel inherited values from the ancient world, placed them into a new setting, reconstructed them, and produced a theological vision which was a "creative advance" over those insights of the predecessor cultures. It would demonstrate the continuity and the intellectual advance Israel's faith had in relation to the worldviews of the ancient Near East. Such, however, is not the role of this present work, rather it should be the goal of another study.

Notes

1. Koch, "Tod," *op. cit.,* pp. 112–114; Reventlow, "Eigenart," *op. cit.,* pp. 199–217; and Stolz, "Monotheismus," *op. cit.,* pp. 143–184.
2. Wright, *Old Testament, op. cit.,* p. 15.
3. Koch, "Tod," *op. cit.,* pp. 112–114.
4. Malamat, "Causality," *op. cit.,* p. 1.
5. Koch, "Tod," *op. cit.,* pp. 112–114.
6. Hayes, *Introduction, op. cit.,* p.136.
7. Cross, *Canaanite Myth, op. cit.,* p. 143.
8. Porter, "Historiography," *op. cit.,* p. 131.
9. Gottwald, "Two Models," *op. cit.,* p. 7, and "Early Israel," *op. cit.,* pp. 32–33.
10. Frick, *Formation, op. cit.,* pp. 193–194.
11. Brueggemann, "Shape," *op. cit.,* pp. 28–46.
12. Eisenstadt, "Axial Age," *op. cit.,* pp. 127–134.
13. Miller, "Israelite Religion," *op. cit.,* p. 207.
14. Koch, "Tod," *op. cit.,* p. 121; Rendtorff, "Entstehung," *op. cit.,* pp. 735–746; Krecher and Müller," "Vergangenheitsinteresse," *op. cit.,* p. 215; and Stolz, "Monotheismus," *op. cit.,* pp. 143–184.
15. Brueggemann, "Shape," *op. cit.,* pp. 35–36; and Miller, "Israelite Religion," *op. cit.,* p. 211.
16. Brueggemann, "Shape," *op. cit.,* pp. 31–40; Ahlström, *Israelites, op. cit.,* p. 97 et passim, stressed Israel's continuity with the past in tension with necessary adaptations for the present.
17. Koch, "Tod," *op. cit.,* pp. 112–114.
18. Benedikt Hartmann, "Monotheismus in Mesopotamien?," *Monotheismus, op. cit.,* pp. 49–79; and Erik Hornung, "Monotheismus im pharaonischen Ägypten," *Monotheismus, op. cit.,* pp. 83–96.
19. Weber, *Judaism, op. cit.,* pp. xvii–xix, 7–8, 252–263; Davisson and Harper, *Ancient World, op. cit.,* pp. 30–85; and Gnuse, *Steal, op. cit.,* pp. 55–56.
20. Frankfort, "The Emancipation of Thought from Myth," *Before Philosophy, op. cit.,* pp. 237–263, made similar observations about the Greeks.
21. Frick, *Formation, op. cit.,* pp. 13–204, described the hypothet-

149

ical collapse of Bronze Age Society using social-scientific models and theoretically projected the reconstruction of Israelite society out of this collapse; and Hopkins, *Highlands, op. cit.,* pp. 15–275, demonstrated how technology and social cooperation must be combined for agricultural success in the Canaanite highlands.

22. Kulke, "Background," *op. cit.,* pp. 390–391; Frick, *Formation, op. cit.,* pp.140–141 et passim; and Ahlström, *Israelites, op. cit.,* pp. 1–118.

23. Saggs, *Encounter, op. cit.,* pp. 21–26, 65–66; and Dever, "Cult," *op. cit.,* pp. 578–579.

24. Richard Goldschmidt, *The Material Basis of Evolution* (New Haven: Yale University, 1940), pp. 184–395, was the first scientist to describe the evolutionary process in genetics as "macro-evolution" or "systemic evolution," a process arising from chromosome mutation on a large scale. He perceived that a "threshold for changed action" is reached by successive mutations in the genetic pool, which produces these evolutionary leaps, p. 396. His ideas were refined by Theodosius Dobzhansky, *Genetics and the Origin of Species* (New York: Columbia University, 1937), pp. 15–191, and Dobzhansky, Francisco Ayala, Ledyard Stebbins, and James Valentine, *Evolution* (San Francisco: Freeman, 1977), pp. 20–56. Contemporary genetics texts have built upon and further refined these ideas: Paul Amos Moody, *Introduction to Evolution,* 2nd ed. (New York: Harper and Brothers, 1962), pp. 502–506, described this process as "mega-evolution"; B. J. Williams, *Evolution and Human Origins* (New York: Harper and Row, 1973), pp. 23–84; Monroe Strickberger, *Genetics,* 2nd ed. (New York: Macmillan, 1976), pp. 735–862; and Eldon Gardner and Peter Snustad, *Principles of Genetics,* 6th ed. (New York: John Wiley and Sons, 1981), pp. 533–611. Recent articulations have described the evolutionary model as "punctuated equilibria," a process wherein long periods of stasis are punctuated by rapid evolutionary advance, Niles Eldredge, *Time Frames: The Rethinking of Darwinian Evolution and the Theory of Punctuated Equilibria* (New York: Simon and Schuster, 1985), pp. 13–223, and *Life Pulse: Episodes from the Story of the Fossil Record* (New York: Facts on File, 1987), pp. 1–240.

25. Eli Sagan, *At the Dawn of Tyranny: The Origins of Individualism, Political Oppression, and the State* (New York: Knopf, 1985), pp. 376–380 et passim.

26. Lenski and Lenski, *Human Societies, op. cit.,* pp. 107–189. Similar language was used by biblical scholars: Crüsemann, *Wider-*

stand, op. cit., pp. 201–215; and Frick, *Formation, op. cit.,* pp. 51–204, spoke of "segmentary" societies and "chiefdoms" in regard to Israel.

27. Sagan, *Tyranny, op. cit.,* p. 378.

28. Rendtorff, "Entstehung," *op. cit.,* pp. 735–746; Koch, "Tod," *op. cit.,* p. 121; Reventlow, "Eigenart," *op. cit.,* p. 215; and Stolz, "Monotheismus," *op. cit.,* pp. 143–184.

29. Albrektson, *History, op. cit.,* pp. 93–95, observed that the various ways in which the ancient worldview was said to be cyclic were really inadequate generalizations. Different theories included: 1) The cyclic worldview was created by the natural cycle of the year and cultic festivals, epitomized by the Mesopotamian *akitu* festival. But this was merely an annual cycle, not one which described history or all of reality. 2) The alternating victory and defeat of various empires helped to create cyclic thought and was manifest in the chronicles, an idea proposed by Güterbock, "Tradition," *op. cit.,* pp. 13–15, and Speiser, "Mesopotamia," *op. cit.,* p. 56. But this is merely alternation, not really a true repetitive cycle. 3) The belief that events in history repeated themselves, as witnessed by the use of astrological tables, implied that all of history might repeat itself. But this concept cannot be found clearly articulated in ancient Near Eastern documents.

Bibliography of Works Consulted

A. Books

Ahlström, Gösta, *Who Were The Israelites?* (Winona Lake, Indiana: Eisenbrauns, 1986).

Albrektson, Bertil, *History and the Gods: An Essay on the Idea of Historical Events as Divine Manifestations in the Ancient Near East and in Israel* (Lund: Gleerup, 1967).

Albright, William Foxwell, *From the Stone Age to Christianity: Monotheism and the Historical Process* (Baltimore: Johns Hopkins University, 1940).

Anderson, Bernhard, *Understanding the Old Testament,* 4th ed. (Englewood Cliffs, New Jersey: Prentice-Hall, 1986).

Barr, James, *Biblical Words for Time,* Studies in Biblical Theology, vol. 33 (Naperville, Illinois: Allenson, 1962).

———, *Old and New in Interpretation: A Study of the Two Testaments* (London: SCM, 1982).

———. *The Scope and Authority of the Bible* (Philadelphia: Westminster, 1980).

Boman, Thorleif, *Hebrew Thought Compared with Greek,* trans. Jules Moreau (London: SCM, 1960).

Bream, Howard; Heim, Ralph; and Moore, Carey, eds., *A Light unto My Path: Old Testament Studies in Honor of Jacob M. Myers,* Gettysburg Theological Studies, vol. 4 (Philadelphia: Temple University, 1974).

Breasted, James Henry, *The Dawn of Conscience* (New York: Scribner's, 1933).

———, *Development of Religion and Thought in Ancient Egypt* (New York: Scribner's, 1912).

153

Butterfield, Herbert, *The Origins of History* (New York: Basic Books, 1981).

Cancik, Hubert, *Grundzüge der hethitischen und alttestamentlichen Geschichtsschreibung* (Wiesbaden: Harrassowitz, 1976).

——, *Mythische und historische Wahrheit: Interpretationen zu Texten der hethitischen, biblischen und griechischen Historiographie*, Stuttgarter Bibelstudien, vol. 48 (Stuttgart: Katholisches Bibelwerk, 1970).

Carney, T. F., *The Economy of Antiquity: Controls, Gifts, and Trade* (Lawrence, Kansas: Coronado, 1973).

Childs, Brevard, *Biblical Theology in Crisis* (Philadelphia: Westminster, 1970).

——, *Memory and Tradition in Israel*, Studies in Biblical Theology, vol. 37 (Naperville, Illinois: Allenson, 1962).

Cross, Frank Moore, *Canaanite Myth and Hebrew Epic: Essays in the History of the Religion of Israel* (Cambridge, Massachusetts: Harvard University, 1973).

Crüsemann, Frank, *Der Widerstand gegen das Königtum: Die antiköniglichen Texte des Alten Testamentes und der Kampf um der frühen israelitischen Staat*, Wissenschaftliche Monographien zum Alten und Neuen Testament, vol. 49 (Neukirchen-Vluyn: Neukirchener, 1978).

Cullmann, Oscar, *Christ and Time: The Primitive Christian Conception of Time and History*, trans. Floyd Filson (Philadelphia: Westminster, 1950).

Davisson, William; and Harper, James, *European Economic History*, vol. 1: *The Ancient World* (New York: Appleton-Century-Crofts, 1972).

Dentan, Robert, ed., *The Idea of History in the Ancient Near East*, American Oriental Series, vol. 38 (New Haven: American Oriental Society, 1955).

Dobzhansky, Theodosius, *Genetics and the Origin of Species* (New York: Columbia University, 1937).

——; Ayala, Francisco; Stebbins, Ledyard; and Valentine, James, *Evolution* (San Francisco: Freeman, 1977).

Dodd, Charles Harold, *The Authority of the Bible*, rev. ed. (London: Fontana, 1960).

Eichrodt, Walther, *Theology of the Old Testament,* 2 vols., trans. James Baker (Philadelphia: Westminster, 1961–1967).

Eisenstadt, Shmuel Noah, ed., *The Origins and Diversity of Axial Age Civilizations,* SUNY Series in Near Eastern Studies (Albany, New York: State University of New York, 1986).

Eldredge, Niles, *Life Pulse: Episodes from the Story of the Fossil Record* (New York: Facts on File, 1987).

————, *Time Frames: The Rethinking of Darwinian Evolution and the Theory of Punctuated Equilibria* (New York: Simon and Schuster, 1985).

Eliade, Mircea, *The Myth of the Eternal Return or, Cosmos and History,* trans. Willard Trask, Bollingen Series, vol. 46 (Princeton, New Jersey: Princeton University, 1954).

Ellis, Maria de Jong, *Essays on the Ancient Near East in Memory of Jacob Joel Finkelstein,* Memoirs of the Connecticut Academy of Arts and Sciences, vol. 19 (Hamden, Connecticut: Archon, 1977).

Fohrer, Georg, *History of Israelite Religion,* trans. David Green (Nashville: Abingdon, 1972).

Frankfort, Henri, ed., *Before Philosophy* (Baltimore: Penguin, 1949).

————, *Kingship and the Gods: A Study of Ancient Near Eastern Religion as the Integration of Society and Nature* (Chicago University of Chicago, 1948).

Freedman, David Noel; and Graf, David Frank, *Palestine in Transition: The Emergence of Ancient Israel,* The Social World of Biblical Antiquity Series, vol. 2 (Sheffield, England: Almond, 1983).

Frick, Frank, *The Formation of the State in Ancient Israel: A Survey of Models and Theories,* The Social World of Biblical Antiquity Series, vol. 4 (Sheffield, England: Almond, 1985).

Gardner, Eldon; and Snustad, Peter, *Principles of Genetics,* 6th ed. (New York: John Wiley and Sons, 1981).

Gnuse, Robert, *The Authority of the Bible: Theories of Inspiration, Revelation, and the Canon of Scripture* (New York: Paulist, 1985).

————, *You Shall Not Steal: Community and Property in the Biblical Tradition* (Maryknoll, New York: Orbis, 1985).

Goedicke, Hans; and Roberts, J. J. M., eds., *Unity and Diversity: Essays in the History, Literature, and Religion of the Ancient Near East* (Baltimore: Johns Hopkins University, 1975).

155

Goldschmidt, Richard, *The Material Basis of Evolution* (New Haven: Yale University, 1940).

Gottwald, Norman, ed., *The Bible and Liberation: Political and Social Hermeneutics* (Maryknoll, New York: Orbis, 1983).

————, *The Tribes of Yahweh: A Sociology of Liberated Israel, 1250–1050 B.C.E.* (Maryknoll, New York: Orbis, 1979).

Gurney, Oliver Robert, *The Hittites* (Baltimore: Penguin, 1952).

Guthrie, Harvey, *God and History in the Old Testament* (Greenwich, Connecticut: Seabury, 1960).

Hallo, William; Moyer, James; and Perdue, Leo, eds., *Scripture in Context II: More Essays on the Comparative Method* (Winona Lake, Indiana: Eisenbrauns, 1983).

Hanson, Paul, *Dynamic Transcendence* (Philadelphia: Fortress, 1978).

Hayes, John, *Introduction to the Bible* (Philadelphia: Westminster, 1971).

Hempel, Johannes, *Altes Testament und Geschichte* (Gütersloh: n.p., 1930).

————, *Geschichten und Geschichte im Alten Testament bis zur persischen Zeit* (Gütersloh: n.p., 1964).

Hopkins, David, *The Highlands of Canaan: Agricultural Life in the Early Iron Age,* The Social World of Biblical Antiquity Series, vol. 3 (Sheffield, England: Almond, 1985).

Jacobsen, Thorkild, *The Treasures of Darkness: A History of Mesopotamian Religion* (New Haven: Yale University, 1976).

Jepsen, Alfred, *Die Quellen des Königsbuches* (Halle: Niemeyer, 1956).

Kaufmann, Yehezkel, *The Religion of Israel: From its Beginnings to the Babylonian Exile,* trans. and abr. Moshe Greenberg (New York: Schocken, 1972).

Keel, Othmar, ed., *Monotheismus im Alten Israel und seiner Umwelt,* Biblische Beiträge, vol. 14 (Stuttgart: Katholisches Bibelwerk, 1980).

Knight, Douglas; and Tucker, Gene, eds., *The Hebrew Bible and its Modern Interpreters,* The Bible and its modern interpreters, vol. 1 (Chico, California: Scholars Press, 1985).

Kramer, Samuel Noah, *From the Tablets of Sumer* (Indian Hills, Colorado: Falcon's Wing Press, 1956).

————, *The Sumerians: Their History, Culture, and Character* (Chicago: University of Chicago, 1963).

Lang, Bernhard, ed., *Der einzige Gott: Die Geburt des biblischen Monotheismus* (Munich: Kösel, 1981).

Lenski, Gerhard; and Lenski, Jean, *Human Societies: An Introduction to Macrosociology,* 3rd ed. (New York: McGraw-Hill, 1978).

Lewis, Brian, *The Sargon Legend: A Study of the Akkadian Text and the Tale of the Hero Who was exposed at Birth,* American Schools of Oriental Research Dissertation Series, vol. 4 (Cambridge, Massachusetts: American Schools of Oriental Research, 1980).

Lindblom, Johannes, *Prophecy in Ancient Israel* (London: Blackwell, 1962).

Luckenbill, Daniel David, *Ancient Records of Assyria and Babylonia,* 2 vols. (New York: Greenwood, 1926).

MacRae, George, ed., *Society of Biblical Literature 1976 Seminar Papers* (Missoula, Montana: Scholars Press, 1976).

McCarter, P. Kyle, *I Samuel,* Anchor Bible (Garden City, New York: Doubleday, 1980).

Meyers, Carol; and O'Connor, Michael, eds., *The Word of the Lord Shall Go Forth: Essays in Honor of David Noel Freedman in Celebration of His Sixtieth Birthday,* American Schools of Oriental Research Special Volume Series, vol. 1 (Winona Lake, Indiana: Eisenbrauns, 1983).

Miller, Patrick; and Roberts, J. J. M., *The Hand of the Lord: A Reassessment of the "Ark Narrative" of 1 Samuel,* The Johns Hopkins Near Eastern Studies, ed. Hans Goedicke (Baltimore: Johns Hopkins University, 1977).

Moltmann, Jürgen, *Theology of Hope,* trans. James Leitch (New York: Harper and Row, 1975).

Montgomery, James, *A Critical and Exegetical Commentary on the Books of Kings,* ed. Henry Gehman, International Critical Commentary (New York: Scribners, 1951).

Moody, Paul Amos, *Introduction to Evolution,* 2nd ed. (New York: Harper and Brothers, 1962).

Moran, William, ed., *Toward the Image of Tammuz and Other Essays* (Cambridge, Massachusetts: Harvard University, 1970).

Mowinckel, Sigmund, *He That Cometh* (Oxford, England: Blackwell, 1956).

Noth, Martin, *The Deuteronomistic History,* trans. Ernest Nicholson, Journal for the Study of the Old Testament Supplement Series, vol. 15 (Sheffield, England: JSOT Press, 1981).

————, *A History of Pentateuchal Traditions,* trans. Bernhard Anderson (Englewood Cliffs, New Jersey: Prentice-Hall, 1972).

————, *The Laws in the Pentateuch and other Studies,* trans. Dafydd Rhys Ap-Thomas (Philadelphia: Fortress, 1967).

Pannenberg, Wolfhart, ed., *History as Revelation,* trans. David Granskou (New York: Macmillan, 1968).

Pritchard, James, ed., *Ancient Near Eastern Texts Relating to the Old Testament,* 3rd ed. (Princeton, New Jersey: Princeton University, 1970).

Reventlow, Henning Graf, *Problems of Old Testament Theology in the Twentieth Century* (Philadelphia: Fortress, 1985).

Richardson, Alan, *The Bible in the Age of Science* (Philadelphia: Westminster, 1961).

Sagan, Eli, *At the Dawn of Tyranny: The Origins of Individualism, Political Oppression, and the State* (New York: Knopf, 1985).

Saggs, H. W. F., *The Encounter with the Divine in Mesopotamia and Israel,* Jordan Lectures in Comparative Religion, vol. 12 (London: Athlone, 1978).

————, *The Might that was Assyria* (London: Sidgwick and Jackson, 1984).

Smend, Rudolf, *Elemente alttestamentliche Geschichtsdenken,* Theologische Studien, vol. 95 (Zurich: EVZ, 1968).

Smith, Morton, *Palestinian Parties and Politics That Shaped the Old Testament* (New York: Columbia University, 1971).

Snaith, Norman, *The Inspiration and Authority of the Bible* (London: Epworth, 1956).

Strickberger, Monroe, *Genetics,* 2nd ed. (New York: Macmillan, 1976).

Tadmor, Hayim; and Weinfeld, Moshe, eds., *History, Historiography* and Interpretation: Studies in biblical and cuneiform literatures (Jerusalem: Magnes, 1984).

Van Seters, John, *In Search of History: Historiography in the Ancient World and the Origins of Biblical History* (New Haven: Yale University, 1983).

Voegelin, Eric, *Order and History,* vol. 1: *Israel and Revelation* (Baton Rouge, Louisiana: Louisiana State University, 1956).

Vriezen, Theodore, *An Outline of Old Testament Theology* (Oxford, England: Blackwell, 1958).

———, *The Religion of Ancient Israel,* trans H. Hoskins (Philadelphia: Westminster, 1967).

Weber, Max, *Ancient Judaism,* trans. and ed. Hans Gerth and Don Martindale (Glencoe, Illinois: Free Press, 1952).

Williams, B. J., *Evolution and Human Origins* (New York: Harper and Row, 1973).

Wittfogel, Karl, *Oriental Despotism: A Comparative Study of Total Power* (New Haven: Yale University, 1957).

Wolf, Herbert Marlin, "The Apology of Hattushilis Compared with Other Political Self-Justifications of the Ancient Near East," Ann Arbor, Michigan: University Microfilms, 1967.

Wright, George Ernest, *God Who Acts: Biblical Theology as Recital,* Studies in Biblical Theology, vol. 8 (London: SCM, 1952).

———, *The Old Testament Against Its Environment,* Studies in Biblical Theology, vol. 2 (Chicago: Regnery, 1950).

———, and Fuller, Reginald, *The Book of the Acts of God,* (Garden City, New York: Doubleday, 1957).

Zeitlin, Irving, *Ancient Judaism* (Cambridge, England: Polity, 1984).

B. Articles

Anderson, Bernhard, "Mendenhall Disavows Paternity: Says He Didn't Father Gottwald's Marxist Theory," *Bible Review* 2, #2 (Summer, 1986): 46–49.

Barr, James, "The Interpretation of Scripture: II. Revelation Through History in the Old Testament and in Modern Theology," *Interpretation* 17 (1963): 193–205.

————, "The Problem of Old Testament Theology and the History of Religion," *Canadian Journal of Theology* 3 (1957): 141–149.

————, "Revelation in History," *Interpreter's Dictionary of the Bible, Supplement,* ed. Keith Crim (Nashville: Abingdon, 1976).

Baumgärtel, Friedrich, "Das Offenbarungszeugnis des Alten Testaments im Lichte der religionsgeschichtlich-vergleichenden Forschung," *Zeitschrift für Theologie und Kirche* 64 (1967): 393–422.

————, "Der Tod des Religionsstifters," *Kerygma und Dogma* 9 (1963): 223–233.

Biggs, Robert, "More Babylonian Prophecies," *Iraq* 29 (1967): 117–132.

Bleeker, C. J., "Review of Bertil Albrektson, History and the Gods," *Bibliotheca Orientalis* 26 (1969): 228–229.

Brinkman, J. A. "Through a Glass Darkly: Esarhaddon's Retrospects on the Downfall of Babylon," *Journal of the American Oriental Society* 103 (1983): 35–42.

Brueggemann, Walter, "A Shape for Old Testament Theology, I: Structural Legitimation," *Catholic Biblical Quarterly* 47 (1985): 28–46.

Brundage, Burr, "The Birth of Clio: A Resume and Interpretation of Ancient Near Eastern Historiography," *Teachers of History: Essays in Honor of Laurence Bradford Packard,* ed. Stuart Hughes (Ithaca: Cornell University, 1954).

Bull, Ludlow, "Ancient Egypt," *The Idea of History in the Ancient Near East,* ed. Robert Dentan.

Burrows, Millar, "Ancient Israel," *The Idea of History in the Ancient Near East,* ed. Robert Dentan.

Chaney, Marvin, "Ancient Palestinian Peasant Movements and the Formation of Premonarchic Israel," *Palestine in Transition,* eds. David Noel Freedman and David Frank Graf.

————, "Systemic Study of the Israelite Monarchy," *Semeia* 37 (1986): 53–76.

Curtis, John Briggs, "A Suggested Interpretation of the Biblical Philosophy of History," *Hebrew Union College Annual* 34 (1963): 115–123.

Dever, William, "Material Remains and the Cult in Ancient Israel:

An Essay in Archaeological Systematics," *The Word of the Lord Shall Go Forth,* ed. Carol Meyers and Michael O'Connor.

Dinkler, Erich, "Earliest Christianity," *The Idea of History in the Ancient Near East,* ed. Robert Dentan.

Drews, Robert, "Sargon, Cyrus and Mesopotamian Folk History," *Journal of Near Eastern Studies* 33 (1974): 387–393.

Eichrodt, Walther, "Offenbarung und Geschichte im Alten Testament," *Theologische Zeitschrift* 4 (1948): 322–329.

Eisenstadt, Shmuel Noah, "The Axial Age Breakthrough in Ancient Israel," *The Origins of Diversity of Axial Age Civilizations,* ed. Shmuel Noah Eisenstadt.

Evans, Carl, "Naram-Sin and Jeroboam: The Archetypal Unheilsherrscher in Mesopotamian and Biblical Historiography," *Scripture in Context II,* eds. William Hallo, James Moyer, and Leo Perdue.

Falkenstein, Adam, "Fluch über Akkade," *Zeitschrift für Assyriologie* 57 (1965): 43–124.

Fensham, Charles, "Widow, Orphan, and the Poor in Ancient Near Eastern Legal and Wisdom Literature," *Journal of Near Eastern Studies* 21 (1962): 129–139.

Finkelstein, Jacob Joel, "Mesopotamian Historiography," *Proceedings of the American Philosophical Society* 107 (1963): 461–472.

———, "The So-called 'Old Babylonian Kutha Legend,' " *Journal of Cuneiform Studies* 11 (1957): 83–88.

Fohrer, Georg, "Prophetie und Magie," *Zeitschrift für die alttestamentliche Wissenschaft* 78 (1966): 25–47.

Frankfort, Henri, "The Emancipation of Thought from Myth," *Before Philosophy,* ed. Henri Frankfort.

Gese, Hartmut, "The Idea of History in the Ancient Near East and the Old Testament," *The Bultmann School of Biblical Interpretation: New Directions?,* ed. Robert Funk, Journal for Theology and the Church, vol. 1 (New York: Harper and Row, 1965).

Gilkey, Langdon, "Cosmology, Ontology, and the Travail of Biblical Language," *Journal of Religon* 41 (1961): 194–205.

Goetze, Albrecht, "The Hittites and Syria," *The Cambridge Ancient History,* vol. 2, part 2: *History of the Middle East and the Aegean*

161

Region c. 1380–1000 B.C., eds. I.E.S. Edwards, N. G. L. Hammond, C. J. Gadd, and E. Sollberger (Cambridge, England: Cambridge University, 1975).

———, "An Old Babylonian Prayer of the Divination Priest," *Journal of Cuneiform Studies* 22 (1968): 25–29.

Goossens, Godefroid, "La philosophie de l'histoire dans l'Ancien Orient," *Sacra Pagina,* 2 vols., eds. Joseph Coppens, Albert Descamps, and Edouard Nassaux, Bibliotheca ephemeridum theologicarum lovaniensium, vols. 12–13 (Gembloux: Duculot, 1959).

Gottwald, Norman, "Early Israel and 'the Asiatic Mode of Production' in Canaan," *Society of Biblical Literature 1976 Seminar Papers,* ed. George MacRae.

———, "Early Israel and the Canaanite Socio-economic System," *Palestine in Transition,* eds. David Noel Freedman and David Frank Graf.

———, "The Participation of Free Agrarians in the Introduction of Monarchy to Ancient Israel: An Application of H. A. Landsberger's Framework for the Analysis of Peasant Movements," *Semeia* 37 (1986): 77–106.

———, "Social Matrix and Canonical Shape," *Theology Today* 42 (1985): 307–321.

———, "The Theological Task after Tribes of Yahweh," *The Bible and Liberation,* ed. Norman Gottwald.

———, "Two Models for the Origins of Ancient Israel: Social Revolution or Frontier Development," *The Quest for the Kingdom of God: Studies in Honor of George E. Mendenhall,* eds. Herbert Huffmon, Frank Spina, and Alberto Green (Winona Lake, Indiana: Eisenbrauns, 1983).

Grayson, A. Kirk, "Assyria: Ashur-dan II to Ashur-Nirari V (934–745 B.C.)," *The Cambridge Ancient History,* vol. 3, pt. 1: *The Prehistory of the Balkans; and the Middle East and the Aegean world, tenth to eighth centuries b.c.,* 3rd ed., ed. John Boardman, I. E. S. Edwards, N. G. L. Hammond, and E. Sollberger (Cambridge, England: Cambridge University, 1982).

Güterbock, Hans, "The Deeds of Suppiluliuma as told by his Son, Mursili II," *Journal of Cuneiform Studies* 10 (1956): 41–68, 75–98, 107–130.

———, "Die historische Tradition und ihre literarische Gestaltung bei Babyloniern und Hethitern bis 1200," *Zeitschrift für Assyriologie* 42 (1938): 45–149.

———, "Hittite Historiography: A Survey," *History, Historiography and Interpretation*, eds. Hayim Tadmor and Moshe Weinfeld.

———, "Sargon of Akkad Mentioned by Hattushili I of Hatti," *Journal of Cuneiform Studies* 18 (1964): 1–6.

Gwaltney, W. C., "The Biblical Book of Lamentations in the Context of Near Eastern Lament Literature," *Scripture in Context II*, eds. William Hallo, James Moyer, and Leo Perdue.

———, "Propaganda and Political Justification in Hittite Historiography," *Unity and Diversity*, eds. Hans Goedicke and J. J. M. Roberts.

Hallo, William, "Individual Prayer in Sumerian: The Continuity of a Tradition," *Essays in Memory of E. A. Speiser*, American Oriental Series, vol. 53 (New Haven: American Oriental Society, 1968).

———, "Sumerian Historiography," *History, Historiography and Interpretation*, eds. Hayim Tadmor and Moshe Weinfeld.

Hanson, Paul, "Jewish Apocalyptic Against Its Near Eastern Environment," *Revue biblique* 78 (1971): 31–58.

Hartmann, Benedikt, "Monotheismus in Mesopotamien?," *Monotheismus im Alten Israel und seiner Umwelt*, ed. Othmar Keel.

Hempel, Johannes, "Altes Testament und Religionsgeschichte," *Theologische Literaturzeitung* 81 (1956): 259–280.

———, "Biblische Theologie und biblische Religionsgeschichte. I. Alten Testament," *Religion in Geschichte und Gegenwart*, 6 vols., 3rd ed., ed. Kurt Galling (Tübingen: Mohr, 1958).

Hesse, Franz, "Bewährt sich eine 'Theologie der Heilstatsachen' am Alten Testament?," *Zeitschrift für die alttestamentliche Wissenschaft* 81 (1969): 1–18.

Hoffner, Harry, "Histories and Historians of the Ancient Near East: The Hittites," *Orientalia* 49 (1980): 283–332.

Hornung, Erick, "Monotheismus im pharaonischen Ägypten," *Monotheismus im Alten Israel und seiner Umwelt*, ed. Othmar Keel.

Hunger, Herbert; and Kaufman, S. A., "A New Akkadian Prophecy Text," *Journal of the American Oriental Society* 95 (1975): 371–375.

Hutter, Manfred, "Bemerkungen über das 'Wort Gottes' bei den Hethitern," *Biblische Notizen* 28 (1985): 17–26.

Jacobsen, Thorkild, "Ancient Mesopotamian Religion: The Central Concerns," *Proceedings of the American Philosophical Society* 107 (1963): 473–484.

————, "Religious Drama in Ancient Mesopotamia," *Unity and Diversity,* eds. Hans Goedicke and J. J. M. Roberts.

Janzen, Gerald, "The Yoke That Gives Rest," *Interpretation* 41 (1987): 256–268.

Koch, Klaus, "Der Tod der Religionsstifters," *Kerygma und Dogma* 8 (1962): 100–123.

————, "Wort und Einheit des Schöpfergottes in Memphis und Jerusalem," *Zeitschrift für Theologie und Kirche* 62 (1965): 251–293.

Kramer, Samuel, "Sumerian Historiography," *Israel Exploration Journal* 3 (1953): 217–232.

Krecher, Joachim; and Müller, Hans Peter, "Vergangenheitsinteresse in Mesopotamien und Israel," *Saeculum* 26 (1975): 13–44.

Kulke, Hermann, "The Historical Background of India's Axial Age," *The Origins and Diversity of Axial Age Civilizations,* ed. Shmuel Noah Eisenstadt.

Lambert, Wilfrid, "Destiny and divine intervention in Babylon and Israel," *Old Testament Studies* 17 (1972): 65–72.

————, "History and the Gods: A Review Article," *Orientalia* 39 (1970): 17–177.

Lemke, Werner, "Revelation through History in Recent Biblical Theology," *Interpretation* 36 (1982): 34–46.

Levenson, Jon, "Is There a Counterpart in the Hebrew Bible to New Testament Antisemitism," *Journal of Ecumenical Studies* 22 (1985): 242–260.

————, "The Temple and the World," *Journal of Religion* 64 (1984): 275–298.

Licht, Joseph, "Biblical Historicism," *History, Historiography and Interpretation,* eds. Hayim Tadmor and Moshe Weinfeld.

Machinist, Peter, "Literature as Politics: The Tukulti-Ninurta Epic and the Bible," *Catholic Biblical Quarterly* 38 (1976): 455–482.

Malamat, Abraham, "Doctrines of Causality in Hittite and biblical Historiography: a parallel," *Vetus Testamentum* 5 (1955): 1–12.

McFadden, Robert, "Micah and the Problem of Continuities and Discontinuities in Prophecy," *Scripture in Context II,* eds. William Hallo, James Moyer, and Leo Perdue.

McKenzie, John, "Aspects of Old Testament Thought," *Jerome Biblical Commentary,* eds. Raymond Brown, Joseph Fitzmeyer, and Roland Murphy (Englewood Cliffs, New Jersey: Prentice-Hall, 1968).

Mendenhall, George, "Ancient Israel's Hyphenated History," *Palestine in Transition,* eds. David Noel Freedman and David Frank Graf.

———, "Migration Theories vs. Culture Change as an Explanation for Early Israel," *Society of Biblical Literature 1976 Seminar Papers,* ed. George MacRae.

Miller, Patrick, "Israelite Religion," *The Hebrew Bible and its Modern Interpreters,* eds. Douglas Knight and Gene Tucker.

Moriarity, Frederick, "Word as Power in the Ancient Near East," *A Light unto My Path,* eds. Howard Bream, Ralph Heim, and Carey Moore.

Mowinckel, Sigmund, "Israelite Historiography," *Annual of the Swedish Theological Institute* 2 (1963): 4–26.

Moyer, James, "Hittite and Israelite Cultic Practices: A Selected Comparison," *Scripture in Context II,* eds. William Hallo, James Moyer, and Leo Perdue.

Murphy, Roland, "Wisdom and Yahwism," *No Famine in the Land: Studies in honor of John L. McKenzie,* eds. James Flanagan and Anita Robinson (Missoula, Montana: Scholars Press, 1975).

Noth, Martin, "Geschichtsschreibung. I. Im Alten Testament," *Religion in Geschichte und Gegenwart,* 6 vols., 3rd ed., ed. Kurt Galling (Tübingen: Mohr, 1958).

———, "History and Word of God in the Old Testament," *The Laws in the Pentateuch and other Studies.*

———, "The Understanding of History in Old Testament Apocalyptic," *The Laws in the Pentateuch and other Studies.*

———, "Von der Knechtgestalt des Alten Testaments," *Evangelische Theologie* 6 (1946/1947): 302–310.

Oden, Robert, "The Deuteronomist as Israel's First Historian," *Interpretation* 38 (1984): 296–299.

Osswald, Eva, "Altorientalische Parallelen zur deuteronomistischen Geschichtsbetrachtung," *Mitteilungen des Instituts für Orientforschung* 15 (1969): 286–296.

Pannenberg, Wolfhart, "Dogmatic Theses on the Doctrine of Revelation," *Revelation as History,* ed. Wolfhart Pannenberg.

———, "Hermeneutics and Universal History," trans. Paul Achtemeier, *History and Hermeneutic,* eds. Robert Funk and Gerhard Ebeling, Journal for Theology and the Church, vol. 4 (New York: Harper and Row, 1967).

———, "Heilsgeschehen und Geschichte," *Kerygma und Dogma* 5 (1959): 218–237, 259–288.

Porter, J. Roy, "Old Testament Historiography," *Tradition and Interpretation: Essays by Members of the Society for Old Testament Study,* ed. George Anderson (Oxford, England: Clarendon, 1979).

———, "Pre-Islamic Arabic Historical Traditions and the Early Historical Narratives of the Old Testament," *Journal of Biblical Literature* 87 (1968): 17–26.

Rad, Gerhard von, "Theologische Geschichtsschreibung im Alten Testament," *Theologische Zeitschrift* 4 (1948): 166–176.

———, "Typological Interpretation of the Old Testament," trans. John Bright, *Essays on Old Testament Hermeneutics,* ed. Claus Westermann (Atlanta: John Knox, 1963).

Rendtorff, Rolf, "The Concept of Revelation in Ancient Israel," *Revelation as History,* ed. Wolfhart Pannenberg.

———, "Die Entstehung der israelitischen Religion als religionsgeschichtliches und theologisches Problem," *Theologische Literaturzeitung* 88 (1963): 735–746.

———, "Hermeneutik des Alten Testaments als Frage nach Geschichte," *Zeitschrift für Theologie und Kirche* 57 (1960): 27–40.

———, "Mose als Religionsstifter?," *Gesammelte Studien sum Alten Testament* (Munich: n.p., 1975).

Rendtorff, Trutz, "The Problem of Revelation in the Concept of the Church," *Revelation as History,* ed. Wolfhart Pannenberg.

Reventlow, Henning Graf, "Die Eigenart des Jahweglaubens als geschichtliches und theologisches Problem," *Kerygma und Dogma* 20 (1974): 199–217.

Roberts, J. J. M., "The Ancient Near Eastern Environment," *The Hebrew Bible and its Modern Interpreters,* eds. Doug Knight and Gene Tucker.

——, "Divine Freedom and Cultic Manipulation in Israel and Mesopotamia," *Unity and Diversity,* eds. Hans Goedicke and J. J. M. Roberts.

——, "Myth Versus History: Relaying the Comparative Foundations," *Catholic Biblical Quarterly* 38 (1976): 1–13.

——, "Nebuchadnezzar I's Elamite Crisis in Theological Perspective," *Essays on the Ancient Near East,* ed. Maria de Jong Ellis.

——, "The Religio-Political Setting of Psalm 47," *Bulletin of the American Schools of Oriental Research* 22 (1976): 129–132.

Rowton, Michael B. "Chronology. II. Ancient Western Asia," *The Cambridge Ancient History,* vol. 1, pt. 1: *Prolegomena and Prehistory,* 3rd ed., eds. I. E. S. Edwards, C. J. Gadd, and N. G. L. Hammond (Cambridge, England: Cambridge University, 1970).

Schmid, Hans Heinrich, "Das alttestamentliche Verständnis von Geschichte in seinem Verhältnis zum gemeinorientalischen Denken," *Wort und Dogma* 13 (1975): 9–21.

Simpson, Cuthbert, "An Inquiry into the Biblical Theology of History," *Journal of Theological Studies* 12 (1961): 1–13.

——, "Old Testament Historiography and Revelation," *Hibbert Journal* 56 (1957/1958): 319–332.

Smith, Morton, " The Common Theology of the Ancient Near East," *Journal of Biblical Literature* 71 (1952): 135–147.

——, "The Present State of Old Testament Studies," *Journal of Biblical Literature* 88 (1969): 19–35.

Soggin, Alberto, "Geschichte, Historie und Heilsgeschichte im Alten Testament," *Theologische Literaturzeitung* 89 (1964): 721–736.

Speiser, Ephraim, "Ancient Mesopotamia," *The Idea of History in the Ancient Near East,* ed. Robert Dentan.

——, "The Biblical Idea of History in its Common Near Eastern Setting," *Israel Exploration Journal* 7 (1957): 201–216.

Stolz, Fritz, "Monotheismus in Israel," *Monotheismus im Alten Israel und seiner Umwelt,* ed. Othmar Keel.

Stuart, Douglas, "The Sovereign's Day of Conquest," *Essays in Honor of George Ernest Wright,* eds. Edward Campbell and Robert Boling (Missoula, Montana: Scholars Press, 1976).

Tadmor, Hayim, "Observations on Assyrian Historiography," *Essays on the Ancient Near East,* ed. Maria de Jong Ellis.

Talmon, Shemaryahu, "The Comparative Method in Biblical Interpretation: Principles and Problems," *Congress Volume: Göttingen, 1977,* Vetus Testamentum Supplements, vol. 29 (Leiden: Brill, 1978).

"Theological Issues in The Tribes of Yahweh by N. K. Gottwald: Four Critical Reviews," *The Bible and Liberation,* ed. Norman Gottwald.

Toombs, Lawrence, "Baal, Lord of the Earth: The Ugaritic Baal Epic," *The Word of the Lord Shall Go Forth,* eds. Carol Meyers and Michael O'Connor.

Uffenheimer, Benjamin, "Myth and Reality in Ancient Israel," *The Origins and Diversity of Axial Age Cvilizations,* ed. Shmuel Noah Eisenstadt.

Vawter, Bruce, "History and Kerygma in the Old Testament," *A Light unto My Path,* eds. Howard Bream, Ralph Heim, and Carey Moore.

Weinfeld, Moshe, "Divine Intervention in War in Ancient Israel and in the Ancient Near East," *History, Historiography and Interpretation,* eds. Hayim Tadmor and Moshe Weinfeld.

Weippert, Manfred, "Fragen des israelitischen Geschichtsbewusstseins, *Vetus Testamentum* 23 (1973): 415–442.

Westermann, Claus, "Sinn und Grenze religionsgeschichtlicher Parallelen," *Theologische Literaturzeitung* 90 (1965): 419–496.

White, John, "Universalism of History in Deutero-Isaiah," *Scripture in Context: Essays on the Comparative Method,* eds. Carl Evans, William Hallo, and John White, Pittsburg Theological Monograph Series, vol. 34 (Pittsburg: Pickwick, 1980).

Widengren, George, "Yahweh's Gathering of the Dispersed," *In the Shelter of Elyon: Essays on Ancient Palestinian Life and Literature in Honor of Gösta W. Ahlström,* eds. Boyd Barrick and John

Spencer, Journal for the Study of the Old Testament Supplement Series, vol. 31 (Sheffield, England: JSOT Press, 1984).

Wildberger, Hans, "Auf dem Wege zu einer biblischen Theologie," *Evangelische Theologie* 19 (1959): 70–90.

Wilkens, Ulrich, "The Understanding of Revelation with the History of Primitive Christianity," *Revelation as History,* ed. Wolfhart Pannenberg.

Wilson, John, "Egypt," *Before Philosophy,* ed. Henri Frankfort.

Wolff, Hans Walter, "The Interpretation of the Old Testament: IV. The Hermeneutics of the Old Testament," trans. Keith Crim, *Interpretation* 15 (1961): 439–472.

Wright, George Ernest, "From the Bible to the Modern World," *Biblical Authority for Today,* eds. Alan Richardson and Wolfgang Schweitzer (London: SCM, 1951).

———, "How did Early Israel differ from her Neighbors," *Biblical Archaeologist* 6 (1943): 1–10, 13–20.

———, "Reflections concerning Old Testament theology," *Studia Biblica et Semitica,* eds. W. C. van Unnik and A. S. van der Woude (Wageningen: Veenman en Zonen, 1966).

Wyatt, Nicolas, "Some Observations on the Idea of History Among the West Semitic Peoples," *Ugarit Forschungen* 11 (1979): 825–832.

Zevit, Ziony, "Deuteronomistic Historiography in I Kings 12–2 Kings 17 and the Reinvestiture of the Israelian Cult," *Journal for the Study of the Old Testament* 32 (1985): 57–73.

Author Index

171

172

174

Subject Index

175

pastoralist or herding society, 126–127, 129, 142
Pentateuch, 36, 95, 158, 165
peripheral culture, 125–126, 142
Persia, Persians, 126, 143, 156
Philistia, Philistines, 16
"Plague Prayer of Mursilis II", 56, 65, 86
polytheism, 13–18, 90, 101, 102, 142, 148
Priestly Editors, 62, 79
Primeval History (Genesis 2–11), 26
"Prism Inscription", 70
"Proclamation of Telepinus", 56, 65
"Prophetic Speech of Marduk", 87
Psalms, 1, 25, 74, 75, 80
Ptah, 63, 75, 147
punctuated equilibria (biological theory), 150, 155

redistributive economies, 131
Resurrection, 1, 23
"Ritual Before Battle", 55–56

Sabbath, 76
Samuel, books of, 51, 86, 92, 94, 157
Sargon of Akkad, 39, 49, 50, 51, 65, 87, 96, 119, 161, 163
Saul, 65, 86
Sefire Treaties, 40
segmentary society, 127, 151
Sennacherib, 70
Seth, 142, 147
Shalmaneser, 58
Shamash, 70
Shamshi-Adad V, 94
Solomon, 46
status redistributive economies, 131

storehouse economies, 131, 143
Succession Narrative (II Samuel), 61
Sumer, Sumerians, 37, 49, 54, 67, 69–70, 75, 78, 82, 157
"Sumerian King List", 34
Suppiluliuma, 42, 50, 162–163
sympathetic magic, 15, 17, 29, 73–74, 146
"Synchronistic Chronicles", 38
"Synchronistic History", 38–39
Syria, Syro-Palestine, 40, 50, 56

"Tablets of Destiny", 61
Telepinus, 42, 65, 89, 108
Temple in Jerusalem, 65, 66, 79, 87, 114, 118
Teshub, 56
"Testament of Hattushilis I", 42
Tetrateuch, 89
Third Dynasty of Ur, 37, 55, 70
Thucydides, 12–13
Tiglath-Pileser I, 57, 58, 70
Tukulti-Ninurta I, 48, 56, 95, 118
"Tukulti-Ninurta Epic", 57, 60, 65, 68, 69, 86, 95, 164
Tushratta, 56
Tuthmosis III, 58, 89

Ugarit, 40
Umma, 54, 69
United Monarchy of Israel, 46, 60
universalism, 92
Ur, 37, 55, 70
Uruk, 58
Urukagina, 70
Utu, 58
Utuhegal, 58

"Weidner Chronicle", 11, 37, 39, 44, 61, 65, 87
Weltgeschichte, 1, 25